100 Fas
LONDONERS

EDITED BY MICHAEL BAKER
AND HILARY BATES NEARY

James Lorimer & Company Ltd., Publishers
Toronto

James Lorimer & Company Ltd acknowledges the support of the Culture Division, Nova Scotia Department of Tourism, Culture and Heritage. We acknowledge the financial support of the Government of Canada through the Book Publishing Industry Development Program (BPIDP) for our publishing activities.

We acknowledge the support of the Canada Council for the Arts for our publishing program.

ONTARIO ARTS COUNCIL
CONSEIL DES ARTS DE L'ONTARIO

Le Conseil des Arts | The Canada Council
du Canada | for the Arts

Library and Archives Canada Cataloguing in Publication

Baker, Michael, 1959 Oct. 5-
    100 fascinating Londoners / Michael Baker and Hilary Bates Neary.

ISBN10: 1-55028-882-2
ISBN13: 978-1-55028-882-7

    1. London (Ont.)—Biography. 2. London (Ont.)—History.
I. Neary, Hilary Bates, 1946- II. Title: One hundred fascinating Londoners.

FC3099.L65Z48 2005   971.3'26'0099   C2005-903277-4

James Lorimer & Company Ltd., Publishers
35 Britain Street
Toronto, Ontario M5A 1R7
www.lorimer.ca

TABLE OF CONTENTS

PHOTO CREDITS

Peter Adams: p 10

Kevin Bice: p 70

Campbell family: p 86

William Casler: p 103

Clark, Sharon, *Eminent Women of Grey County*. Owen Sound, Ontario: Grey County Historical Society, 1977: pp 63L, 63R

Karin Cochran: p113

W. Curtin: p 106

Walter Dixon in Mayfair, 1936, Toronto Reference Library: pp 78, 96

Danse Canada Dance: p 75B, 102T

Glen Curnoe: p 12

Elgin County Archives, Scott-Sefton Collection, Box 100-#97253: p 46

Huron University College p 15

Ivey Family London Room, London Public Library: pp 9,18, 24T, 41T, 41B, 43, 54, 55, 65, 67, 80T, 107

Elizabeth Lawson, p 101

London Free Press: pp 68, 72, 75T, 76, 77, 81, 83, 84, 90, 91, 94T, 94B, 97, 98, 99, 102B, 104T, 104B, 105, 109B, 110, 114

London Free Press Collection of Photographic Negatives, The University of Western Ontario Archives: pp 16, 59T, 64T, 64B, 80B, 87, 92, 108, 112, 115

Victor Long, portrait, in Wells, Eric. *Winnipeg: Where the New West Begins*, Burlington, Ontario: Windsor Publications, 1982: p 17

Maridon Miller in Miller, Orlo. *This Was London: The First Two Centuries*. Westport, Ontario: Butternut Press, 1988: p 20

Paul Mombourquette in the *London and Middlesex Historian*, Volume 19, Autumn, 1992: p 53T

Matthews Hall: p 60

McIntosh Gallery, The University of Western Ontario: p 74

Museum London: pp 21B, 22, 23T, 24B, 25, 26, 28, 29, 31, 32, 33B, 33T, 34, 36, 37, 39, 42, 47T, 47B, 48, 53B, 61, 66, 69B, 89, 100

Museum of the City of New York: p 27

James Reaney: p 49

Richmond family: p 109T

Somerville family: p 93

St. Peter's Seminary: p 51

John Tamblyn: pp 7, 14, 23B, 40, 50, 57, 58, 73, 88

J. Wandesforde, portrait, Eldon House, City of London Collection, Gift of Mr. A. Little: p 21T

The University of Western Ontario Archives: pp 8, 13, 35, 38, 52, 59L, 59R, 69T, 95

Women's Christian Association Archives: p 45

INTRODUCTION

A complete dictionary of London biography would fill many volumes. Our challenge when we began this project was to select just 100 or so of the thousands of memorable people who have lived within a few kilometres of the forks of the Thames from before the city's founding to the present day. We have chosen our 100 with an eye to balance, contrast, and surprise. People from all walks of life, the humble to the grand, and from professions and avocations ranging from architect to zoologist, are represented in these pages. Our pursuit of these individuals will take you to the penal colony of Van Diemen's Land; to Selma, Alabama, to march alongside Dr. Martin Luther King Jr.; to home plate in the 1909 World Series; to the trenches of war-torn France; and even to the banks of the river Tay, for the last fatal duel in Canada.

Our diverse characters are linked by one thing: they share London as their one-time home or final resting place. Some of their stories intersect. Charles Henry Ivey successfully appealed Joseph Saunby's case against the City of London to the Judicial Committee of the Privy Council, and William Robinson designed the manse of First-St. Andrew's Presbyterian Church where Marian Keith wrote so many of her books. We can enjoy imagining other ways in which these characters' paths may have crossed: could Slippery Jack have intruded upon the slumbers of Amelia Harris or Emma Hunt? How many children of the Londoners profiled here did Kate Matthews teach? Which of them studied dance with Bernice Harper? The trailblazing photographer Jeanne Graham could have taken many shots of musician Gordon Jeffery or of Premier John Robarts. Who among these Londoners sat in Shack Martin's barber's chair? We hope these people's stories will whet your appetite to discover more about our former citizens and their myriad interests and accomplishments.

The biographies of our Londoners are arranged by their year of death, giving our book a kind of chronological narrative. Their surnames appear alphabetically in bold type in the index.

In 2003, we edited *London Street Names*, also published by James Lorimer & Company. That book profiled many Londoners who left their names on local roads. Many who wrote for our first collaborative book contributed to this one as well, but we have also found new recruits for the genre of biography. In all, fifty-nine local writers are represented here, all of whom reflect our fascination with the personalities who shape history. We deeply appreciate the enthusiasm our contributors have demonstrated through their research and writing, and we thank them most sincerely. For their assistance to all of us, we thank Arthur McClelland and the staff of the Ivey Family London Room at the London Public Library, and John Lutman and Theresa Regnier of the J.J. Talman Regional Collection at the University of Western Ontario (UWO).

We are also grateful for the help we received in compiling the illustrations for the book, particularly from Anita McCallum, librarian at the *London Free Press*; Alan Noon, Media Specialist in Photography in the Faculty of Science, UWO; Robert Ballantine at Museum London; and Barry Arnott of the UWO Archives. We likewise received timely assistance from Daniel Holt and Grant Maltman. Many institutions lent visual material or allowed John Tamblyn to photograph their buildings and collections. Friends and family of many of the subjects generously shared photographs and other materials with us, and they too have our sincere thanks. And finally we acknowledge the advice and support of the wonderfully informed Daniel J. Brock.

It is fitting that *100 Fascinating Londoners* be published in 2005, London's sesquicentennial year, and that it play a part in the celebration of a century and a half of our civic life. We invite you to a biographical feast of 100 lives lived in the Forest City.

Michael Baker and Hilary Bates Neary

The Talbot child's grave in Oakland Cemetery, 390 Oxford Street West.

"THE TALBOT TOT"
(LATE 1830S)

On March 27, 2001, excavation on the Talbot Block for what is now the John Labatt Centre halted when workers unearthed a tiny six-sided coffin, beneath a blanket of ash. The bones inside belonged to an 18- to 36-month-old of undetermined sex.

This author set out to identify the parentage of the child, dubbed "the Talbot Tot," before further excavation removed all traces of its grave. Quickly ruled out were settlers who had lived there after London's Great Fire of 1845 (a possible source of the ash). This left two possibilities: merchant Dennis and Jane (Shotwell) O'Brien, who owned the adjacent lot to the north, and grocer John and Mary O'Flynn, who bought the east half of the lot in question in 1839. In the early 1800s it was still common to bury one's kin on one's own property, although London's Roman Catholic church — which both families attended — had its own graveyard by the mid-1830s. The cause of the toddler's death is unknown, but childhood mortality was high in the days before inoculation, a safe public water supply, and an adequate sewer system.

On May 9, 2001, the Rev. Robert Ripley of Metropolitan United Church conducted a private re-interment service in Oakland Cemetery for the unknown child. Five days later Londoners paid their respects at a public service at the church. A bronze plaque marks the child's final resting place.

Dan Brock

EDWARD ALLEN TALBOT
(c. 1796-1839)

An "original thinker and a great projector of new schemes" who claimed a "high literary reputation" in both the Canadas and the British Isles, Edward Allen Talbot died a broken man.

Immigrating to Upper Canada in 1818, he was co-founder, with his father, Richard, of the Protestant Tipperary Irish settlement in London Township. In 1824, his *Five Years' Residence in the Canadas* was published in England. In 1831, he joined forces with Robert Heron of Niagara to publish *The London Sun*, the province's first newspaper west of Ancaster. During this time and for the next several years he continued to expend much time, energy, and his family's money both on his earlier scheme of perpetual motion and now on an improved steam engine which could be used by vehicles on water, road, or rail. In 1834, his "Atmospheric Propelling Engine" became the first invention patented by the Upper Canadian government. Talbot also drew up the charter for the London and Gore Rail Road Company, incorporated that same year.

By this time, however, his newspaper had failed and both he and his wife were teaching school. Over the next few years the family lived in Niagara and London where Talbot continued to teach and practise journalism. His connections with the Reform movement led to his taking leave of London following the Rebellion of 1837. Unfortunately, he was now suffering from alcoholism. Shortly before his death, he sent his wife what little he still possessed, and voluntarily admitted himself into the Lockport, N.Y., poor-house and hospital where he died.

Dan Brock

ELIJAH WOODMAN
(1797-1847)

Elijah Woodman, 1844.

Elijah Crocker Woodman was born in Buxton, Maine, and immigrated to Upper Canada in 1830. He established himself first at Big Otter Creek (near Tillsonburg), where he ran a sawmill and lumber business, and then in London, where he was drawn into radical politics. In June 1838 he was arrested and charged with passing weapons to prisoners jailed in London following the Rebellion of 1837. He was, however, released from detention. In December, he was involved in a failed rebel attack on Windsor from Detroit. Imprisoned again in London, he was sentenced to hang but was ultimately transported to Van Diemen's Land (now Tasmania). He left behind his wife,

Apphia Elden, and four daughters and three sons.

In exile he endured the hardships of the penal system and in 1842 was given a "ticket of leave" and worked as a carpenter and millwright. Pardoned by Queen Victoria on March 1, 1845, he was now able to leave Van Diemen's Land, but he had tuberculosis and was frail and destitute. It took him nearly two years to secure passage to the United States, on the whaler *Young Eagle*. But his health did not withstand the long voyage and on June 13, 1847, he died off the Juan Fernández Islands, near Chile, and was buried at sea.

His eldest daughter, Emeline, married Elijah Leonard Jr., who became one of London's most successful businessmen and politicians. She and her family preserved his papers and thereby ensured that his hard place in the city's history would be well remembered.

Michael DeKay

S.K. Davidson's copy of a painting by Cyrenius Hall of Robert and Hannah Flint in their home that still stands in Springbank Park.

ROBERT AND HANNAH FLINT

(1784–1859) AND (1788–1865)

Robert Flint emigrated in 1834 from Norfolk, England, to what later became Byron; he was joined two years later by his wife Hannah and their four children. Flint constructed distinctive cobblestone structures in the

Byron area, using techniques similar to those he had used for flint buildings in England. His three best-known buildings are St. Anne's Church (c. 1855), his own cottage (c. 1838), and a cottage built at the corner of his farm for his son Pirney (1856; later enlarged). In 1891, the city of London bought the Flint farm as part of London's waterworks system and the developing Springbank Park. Thus the cottages became, and remain, picturesque landmarks within the park landscape.

A valuable legacy of family letters is particularly revealing about the Flints' lives and characters. Hannah is shown to be an astute, well-educated, staunchly upright woman, inclined to be judgmental of others and acutely aware of her own sufferings. When her youngest son, Pirney, returned from seeking gold in California, she claimed to be so distraught at his heavy drinking and low company that she said she "would sooner live in a cave in the earth than live the life [she did]." Robert Flint, in contrast, appears hardworking (despite being lame), uncomplaining, and consistently tolerant. Against Hannah's advice, he insisted on building the house for the wayward Pirney. There Pirney became a conscientious, though feisty, farmer and a devoted husband and father.

Nancy Z. Tausky

Henry Dormer

HENRY EDWARD DORMER
(1844-1866)

London's only candidate for sainthood, a 21-year-old British army ensign, lived in the city for a mere seven months. Before his arrival in London on February 24, 1866, Henry Edward Dormer visited his sister, a Dominican nun at Stone Priory in Staffordshire. Once in London, he wrote his sister that he was a changed man: "From the moment I left Stone, after having had the inestimable blessing of making my peace with God, I have had a kind of resolution in my mind to abandon the world and join a religious order." After his military duties, Dormer could be found in an ecstasy of prayer either at St. Peter's Church, or in the chapel of the Sacred Heart Convent, often all night long. He also began attending selflessly to London's poor and sick. As a result, he contracted typhoid fever, which killed him on October 2, 1866. Dormer had already resigned from the army and was awaiting word about whether he would be accepted into the Dominican friars. As Catholic historian Theodore Smeenk wrote, Dormer's "release from the Army was in the mail and reached London on the morning of his death. He died between the uniform of his Queen and the uniform of his Lord."

Less than two weeks after his death, Father Byrne, the superior of the Dominican friars, wrote to Dormer's parents: "In all the sincerity of my soul I believe, my dear Lord and Lady, that you have brought into the world and reared to manhood a great saint." And so began the famously slow process of canonization, which continues.

Herman Goodden

AMANDA WETHERBEE
(c. 1820–1867)

Amanda Wetherbee was originally buried in the Methodist Cemetery which was located on the site of the present Agriplex Building at Western Fair Grounds. A white marble headstone, carved and placed on her grave by Teale Bros., reads:

IN
Memory of
LAVINIA HERMIONE
GERTRUDE AMANDA
GUELPH
Daughter of George IV
And wife of
Charles Wetherbee
DIED
Jan. 25. 1867.
AE 46 Yrs.

Amanda and Charles Wetherbee moved from the southern United States to the Nilestown area during the American Civil War. Shortly after they

Headstone of Amanda Guelph Wetherbee.

moved to London and lived near Clarence and Hill streets.

Amanda Wetherbee was known to have said that she was a daughter of King George IV. Although unsubstantiated, the enigma of her royal parentage cannot be totally dismissed, because George IV was known to have had many lovers.

The background of "Princess Amanda" was explored in an 1891 *London Free Press* article. A reporter interviewed a woman well acquainted with Mrs Wetherbee who was quoted as saying that "… she appeared to be a most honorable lady and her scant wardrobe certainly gave evidence of better days, being of the finest and most costly texture." She also said that it was rumoured that Amanda Wetherbee was "a real born lady." In the same article, a cemetery official of the time stated that "lots of people made inquiries about that stone."

The Methodist Cemetery was closed in 1874 and the graves were moved to the newly opened Mount Pleasant Cemetery. Amanda's grave was moved in 1879.

The inscription on her headstone remains a mystery.

Glen Curnoe

JOHN WILSON
(1809-1869)

An honest lawyer may be the last person one would expect to fight a fatal duel and win.

John Wilson hailed from Paisley, Scotland. He and his family settled near Perth, Upper Canada. While a law student there in 1833, Wilson killed Robert Lyon in a duel over the honour of Elizabeth Hughes. Charged with murder, Wilson was later acquitted. In 1835 he was called to the bar and married Elizabeth. The couple moved to London, where they raised eight children. Wilson held a succession of offices, including district warden, and solicitor for London. He was known as a "large hearted," able lawyer, affectionately nicknamed "Honest John Wilson." In 1847, he was elected as a Conservative to the Legislative Assembly. He became disillusioned with Tory extremism, however, and allied himself with the Reformers. In 1851, he was defeated by Thomas C. Dixon. Some believed this was owing to his remarks that the Irish weren't fit to carry firearms. Nevertheless, in 1854, he defeated Dixon and stayed in the Legislature until 1857. He was made a Queen's Counsel in 1856 and a judge in 1863.

Perhaps the stress of presiding over the Fenian raid trials shortened his life. But in death, as in life, Wilson was highly regarded. Businesses were

John Wilson telling a story in a sketch by Judge Elliot. Left to right: Lawrence Lawrason, John Wilson, John Harris, and T.W. Shepherd, c. 1845.

closed during his funeral procession: it may have been the largest London had seen up to that time. It was also the last where members of the bar appeared in their robes, a gesture of respect for Honest John Wilson.

Leith Peterson

GEORGE JERVIS GOODHUE
(1799–1870)

Born in Vermont, George J. Goodhue settled in the London area in 1820 as a general merchant and distiller. He relocated to London about 1827, forming a partnership with another merchant, Lawrence Lawrason. When they parted amicably in 1840, Goodhue was rumoured to have received $40,000. After 1840 he concentrated on land speculation, charging interest rates as high as 24 percent, and eventually holding paper on properties in nine neighbouring counties. Goodhue also established connections with the Bank of Upper Canada, of which he was later a director, and was one of the first postmasters in London.

When London was incorporated in 1840, he became its first president.

Politically a liberal, he was appointed to the Legislative Council in 1841, sitting until Confederation.

Goodhue married twice, first to Maria Fullerton of Vermont who died in 1828, and then to Louisa Matthews, daughter of a local reform-oriented family. They had four daughters and two sons.

In a new will made just before his death in January, 1870, Goodhue provided that the bulk of his $650,000 estate would be distributed only after his wife's death. The result was a prolonged legal battle between his executor, H.C.R. Becher, and Goodhue's children, Charles and Mary, who demanded immediate distribution. In the end, Becher's position was upheld and the estate distributed only after Louisa's death in 1880.

Typical of many Upper Canadian merchants, Goodhue was a man of business who thought of little else except business. His harsh tactics made him a legend.

Frederick H. Armstrong

BISHOP BENJAMIN CRONYN
(1802-1871)

A graduate of Trinity College, Dublin, Benjamin Cronyn and several clerical friends emigrated to Canada in 1832. He stopped in London en route to Adelaide Township and was persuaded to stay in the emerging district capital.

St. Paul's Cathedral, Richmond and Queens.

He quickly became rector of St. Paul's and St. John's (Arva) and chaplain to both the local British garrison and the district jail. When southwestern Ontario was separated from the Diocese of Toronto in 1857, Cronyn was elected the first bishop of the new Diocese of Huron. He was the first bishop chosen by election in the worldwide Anglican communion.

Bishop Cronyn portrait, Huron University College common room.

Enviously energetic, Cronyn founded 101 parishes during his episcopate. Strongly low-church (evangelical) in his theology, he came into conflict with the more tractarian (restoring traditional Catholic practices) traditions of Trinity College in Toronto, and founded Huron College in 1863. Graduates of Huron were instrumental in founding Western University in 1878. Cronyn's descendants continued to be prominent in London's business and politics for several generations. The noted actor Hume Cronyn was a great-grandson.

Few physical reminders of Cronyn's once persuasive presence remain. His houses — a rectory on the site later occupied by Mount St. Joseph, another on Queen's Avenue next to St. Paul's Cathedral, and a family home on Dundas near Adelaide Street — have all been demolished. His real monuments are the Anglican Diocese of Huron and Huron University College, where his portrait hangs in the Great Hall.

Douglas Leighton

NOBLE ENGLISH
(c. 1797-1872)

After emigrating from the U.S. to Upper Canada, Noble English married Elizabeth Forsyth. The first of the pioneer couple's 13 children, Robert, was born in 1818. In 1819, Noble obtained a land grant of 100 acres from Col. Thomas Talbot and cleared and farmed the land. The English homestead was built on the north side of the Governor's Road (now Dundas Street). With the purchase of an additional 100 acres of land in 1837, Noble's property was now extended from Dundas north to Central Avenue and from Adelaide Street East to Woodman Avenue. In the mid-1850s he sold some land to Murray Anderson when London began to expand eastward. Noble and Elizabeth were staunch Methodists. Two sons, Wesley and Egerton Ryerson, were named after prominent Methodists; two others, Noble Franklin and John, became ministers. In 1883, a grandson, Rev. Edward, an ordained Anglican priest, became the principal of Hellmuth Ladies' College, London's private school for the higher education of young women.

Elizabeth died in 1864. Noble died in 1872, survived by six children and his second wife Eleanore. Later that year, Samuel Peters Jr. surveyed and subdivided his remaining property into building lots. English Street still bears the family name. Elizabeth Street was named after Noble's wife. Elias Street was named for a son, just as were Timothy Street (now Lorne Avenue), Franklin Street (now Dufferin Avenue) and Lyman Street (now Princess Avenue).

Glen Curnoe

GEORGE LOVELESS
(1797–1874)

Some people are famous because of what they do, others because of what has been done to them. George Loveless was one of the latter. An English labourer and Methodist lay-preacher, he was arrested in 1834 for union organizing in Tolpuddle, Dorsetshire, England. Administering illegal oaths was the formal offence. A misdemeanour at best, the Whig government

George Specht, President, London District Labour Council lays a wreath at the George Loveless headstone, Labour Day, 1957.

chose to prosecute it as a felony. He and five others were sentenced to seven years transportation to Van Diemen's Land (Tasmania). The sentence was probably illegal, and in its severity indefensible. In 1836, the so-called Tolpuddle martyrs were pardoned in response to public pressure. They returned to a hero's welcome. Funds were collected for their relief. At the behest of supporters, Loveless told his story in a short pamphlet, "The Victims of Whiggery."

In 1844, he and four other martyrs immigrated to Canada West, and lived out their lives in quiet obscurity. Loveless bought land in London Township. Prospering as a farmer, he continued to be active as a Methodist lay-preacher and helped found the Siloam Church. The martyrdom long remained a family secret, unknown to his neighbours. His gravestone reads: "These are they which came out of great tribulation and have washed their robes and made them white in the blood of the Lamb." An historical plaque by the Siloam cemetery on Fanshawe Road commemorates his importance in the British labour movement. The gravestone testifies to something else. Had he changed his mind about unions?

Fred Dreyer

FRANCIS EVANS CORNISH
(1831-1878)

Mayor from 1861 to 1865, and one of London's most controversial politicians, Francis Evans Cornish was a hard-drinking, two-fisted master of frontier politics. Charming and intelligent, but frequently impulsive and erratic, Cornish revelled in his roguish reputation. To his many supporters, Cornish was "The Working Man's Friend." His enemies scorned him as a public embarrassment.

Francis Evans Cornish, c.1860.

The son of one of London's first public servants, Cornish studied law and became a Queen's Counsel at the age of 26. He used his connections as a Mason, Orangeman, and Conservative to win a seat on City Council in 1858.

Cornish's voting record on Council was that of a reformer, but his often corrupt political methods and questionable personal life cost him the support of respectable Londoners. After his defeat in 1865, Cornish's marriage collapsed. His political career seemed to be over after he was soundly beaten by John Carling in the 1871 provincial election.

In 1872, Cornish joined the wave of Ontarians seeking opportunity in the new Province of Manitoba. The "wild west" suited Cornish, and he soon became one of Manitoba's most prominent lawyers. Cornish was elected Winnipeg's first mayor in 1874, and won a seat in the provincial legislature a year later.

Cornish's second political career ended abruptly with stomach cancer. He died at the age of 47. Today, Cornish is remembered in his hometown for several scandalous incidents that have become entrenched in local folklore, but his many positive political contributions have now been largely forgotten.

John Mombourquette

Dr. John Salter, c. 1870.

DR. JOHN SALTER
(1802-1881)

Businessman, editor, individualist, pharmacist, sailor, secret philanthropist, student of art and literature, surgeon, thinker, and writer, John Salter was born in London, England. He became an apothecary and for nine years acted as surgeon on ships plying between England and the Caribbean.

Salter came to London in 1835 and worked for Lyman, Farr & Co.'s drug store, then took charge of the drug department in Smith & Moore's general store. He acted as surgeon for the London garrison during the Rebellion of 1837–38. He married Anne Wright of Westminster Township, and opened his own apothecary on Ridout Street. It burned down during the Great Fire of 1845. He rebuilt, at Dundas and Maitland in 1856, and later at Dundas and Clarence. Though not a licensed physician, Salter prescribed treatment, was generally called "doctor," and acted as London's first dentist until Solon Woolverton arrived in 1880.

A well educated man, Salter edited the influential *London Times* for ten years, in which he vigorously promoted his views. A Conservative, he chaired the 1847 meeting where "Honest" John Wilson, later MP for London, entered provincial politics. Until his death Salter promoted social reforms — the abolition of the death penalty, improvement of prison conditions, humane treatment of offenders, and repeal of the Debtors' Act. The "patriarch of druggists" died on April 6, 1881. He had circumnavigated the globe several times but had never been on a railroad car in his life.

Arthur McClelland

"SLIPPERY JACK"
(1881-1889)

In April 1866, someone began breaking into houses in London, but the mysterious burglar took nothing. Variously described as a "lunatic fellow," "Jack Sheppard," "Mysterious Creature," and "The Mysterious," by mid-June the press had settled on the name "Slippery Jack." After several months, the break-ins stopped as suddenly as they had started.

Then, in a September 1867 issue of the *Weekly Advertiser*, Slippery Jack claimed he had made a $500 wager that within a year he would enter 60 houses — five a month — without having his identity suspected. He then confirmed that he had won his bet.

It was only in October 1888 that Jack's identity was revealed to the public, again through the *Advertiser*. In fact, there were *two* Slippery Jacks, Bill Simmons, who "could climb up a wall almost," and John Talbot Darnley Talbot-Crosbie, who "was a character." Both were members of London's "Hellfriar Club," a men's social club formed in 1863. Simmons was a cabinetmaker and Talbot-Crosbie was a lieutenant in the 60th Regiment then stationed in London.

Drawing of "Slippery Jack" by Maridon Miller.

According to the informant, "They used to go out turn about, and when one was out the other would always manage to be at a ball or party somewhere, so as he wouldn't be suspected. If Talbot-Crosby was dancing all night while Slippery Jack was house-breaking it couldn't be him. It was the same with Simmons." Simmons appears to have died in 1881, leaving a widow. Talbot-Crosbie returned to the family estate in Ireland, and died in 1899.

Dan Brock

AMELIA HARRIS
(1798–1882)

Many shapers and builders of Canada came and went through the hospitable doors of Amelia Harris's home, Eldon House. As a result, Amelia's witty diary observations covered not only her family, but also many leaders of the Victorian era. She described Prime Minister John A. Macdonald as a man who "… condemns and despises what in drunkenness and debauchery he gives himself up to." Excerpts from Amelia's diaries were published by the Champlain Society in 1994 and delight readers to this day.

Amelia Harris, c. 1860.

Amelia Harris was the daughter of United Empire Loyalist, Samuel Ryerse. The Americans burned her family farm near Long Point during the War of 1812. In 1815, she married Royal Navy Master John Harris and they settled in Kingston. Amelia assisted her husband with a hydrographic survey of the Great Lakes, performing such tasks as tracing the Thousand Islands on oil paper. Her husband referred to her as "Deputy Assistant Marine Surveyor and Housekeeper to the Establishment."

Several years later they returned to Long Point and John was named District Treasurer, which took them to the new district seat, London, in 1834. The Harrises' three surviving sons became lawyers. Four of their seven daughters married British Army officers stationed in London. Amelia managed this large brood by preparing entries in her diary and then leaving it out for family members to read. She continued these notations from 1857 until within weeks of her death. Her character was portrayed in three episodes of CBC TV's *Canada: A People's History.*

Leith Peterson

SAMUEL PETERS JR.
(1822–1882)

Samuel Peters Jr. immigrated to Canada West (Ontario) from Torquay, England, and settled in London in about 1843, where he gained prominence as an architect, engineer, and surveyor. His surveyor's notebooks, compiled c. 1843-1874, contain a wealth of historical material.

Samuel Peters Jr.

He was appointed town engineer in 1852 and oversaw the building of sewers. When the city of London was incorporated in 1855, he became city engineer and held that position for a year. He designed the city hall that stood on the west side of Richmond Street between Dundas and King. Having surveyed much of what is now central London, in 1856 he produced a map for publication in the city's first directory.

King Street looking west towards Talbot Street, c. 1910. Rightmost is the original market building, c. 1854, designed by Samuel Peters Jr.

For many years, he was a trustee of the North Street Wesleyan Methodist Church. In 1854, he surveyed and drew the plan for the congregation's new cemetery, now the site of the Agriplex Building at the Western Fair Grounds.

In 1882, Peters died of typhoid that he contracted while making a survey for the projected London and Port Burwell Railway. He was buried in Mount Pleasant cemetery, which he had surveyed and designed in the mid-1870s.

Two of the buildings that Peters designed still stand: Grosvenor Lodge (1017 Western Road), built in 1853 for his uncle and namesake, now the London Regional Resource Centre for Heritage and the Environment, and Askin Street Methodist Church, built in 1880, now Wesley-Knox United Church.

Glen Curnoe

HENRY CORRY ROWLEY BECHER
(1817-1885)

Some political careers have been ruined by scandal or drink, but Henry Corry Rowley Becher saw his political aspirations destroyed by a dance. Becher's law practice and investments flourished, but his dream of going to Parliament floundered. His downfall was precipitated by a ball to honour Edward, Prince of Wales, who visited London in 1860. Held in the new Tecumseh House Hotel, four hundred of London's elite were invited as guests. As master of ceremonies, Becher was responsible for ensuring that the prince danced with the ladies who had been selected by the ball's organizing committee. Fathers and husbands of those not on the Prince's dance card threatened and almost attacked Becher. Within days, the local newspaper criticized his management of the ball. The following year he lost the Tory nomination for East Middlesex. Though supported by John A. Macdonald himself, he blamed his defeat on the offence taken by many former friends and neighbours.

Henry C.R. Becher

Becher had emigrated from England in 1835, boarding with the Harris family at Eldon House. He articled with John Wilson and was soon registrar of the Surrogate Court of Middlesex County. One of the finest legal minds in the province, he assembled many important clients, including the Great Western Railway, and in the course of his career settled the large and controversial estates of Col. Thomas Talbot and George J. Goodhue. His Gothic villa, Thornwood, built in the 1840s, remained in the Becher family until the 1980s, and still stands on St. George Street. His diaries present a wonderful picture of early life in London, Ontario.

Sportsman, author, and traveller, Becher is credited with introducing cricket to London, and crossed the Atlantic 22 times, dying in England.

Alice M. Gibb

Thornwood, 329 St. George Street.

SALLIE HOLMAN
(1852-1888)

Sallie Holman,
c. 1880.

George Holman immigrated with his family to London from Margate, England, at the age of 12. Already stage-struck, the young lad realized during a stopover in New York City that he must go there to achieve his theatrical dreams and left the family's Simcoe Street home to do just that three years later. Touring as a musical entertainer with various American companies over the next decade, George met and married divorced singer and actress Harriet Phillips in 1849.

Their first child, Sallie Holman, was born in Lynn, Massachusetts. Nine years later, she and her three siblings made their stage debut in Indianapolis in an early version of the family-run troupe which made light comic opera their specialty. From that day until her death from consumption at the age of 36, Sallie would be the star attraction of the Holman Opera Company, regularly playing theatres in Toronto, Montreal, Boston, New York City and Washington and winning armies of ardent male admirers, including Ulysses S. Grant.

Though the Holmans spent most months of the year on tour, they also operated their own opera house, first in Toronto and then in London at the northwest corner of Richmond and York streets from 1873 to 1881. They achieved the commercial and critical peak of their long career with their 1879 production of Gilbert & Sullivan's *HMS Pinafore*. Theirs was the first Canadian production of that work, and it was widely considered the best in all North America.

Herman Goodden

GEORGE F. DURAND
(1850-1889)

George Durand,
c. 1875.

At the time of his premature death in 1889, the *London Advertiser* proudly claimed that local architect George F. Durand "was acknowledged to be the best designer in the Dominion." The son of prominent London contractor James Durand, George had apprenticed as an architect with William Robinson, then joined Thomas Fuller (later chief architect to the Dominion of Canada) in overseeing the construction of the massive, ornate New York State Capitol in Albany. After returning to London, Durand became a senior partner in Robinson's firm.

His partners shared a strong interest in engineering, but Durand usually retained artistic control of his firm's productions. A symbolic self-portrait in one of his earliest surviving drawings, for the Federal Bank once on the northwest corner of Dundas and Richmond streets (1878–79), shows the architect in the medieval tights and tunic adopted by self-conscious aesthetes of the period. His designs typically employ the elaborate, eclectic vocabulary associated with the High Victorian Gothic, Second Empire, Queen Anne, and Romanesque Revival styles, but in his hands their characteristic verbosity is organized into controlled, balanced, carefully articulated sentences.

Under his leadership, the firm attracted clients from the Toronto area, as well as throughout southwestern Ontario. Among the firm's commissions were the Perth County Buildings in Stratford, Upper Canada College in Toronto, numerous southwestern Ontario churches; and in London, the Grand Opera House and Masonic Temple; the London East Town Hall; the Colborne Street Methodist (now United) Church; Oakwood, a palatial residence for Benjamin Cronyn, and Waverley, a stately home for Cronyn's brother-in-law. Charles Goodhue.

Nancy Z. Tausky

ELIJAH LEONARD JR.
(1814-1891)

An ingenious Yankee, Elijah Leonard Jr. built western Ontario's first steam engine. Leonard was born near Syracuse, New York, and moved in 1830 with his family to Normandale, near Long Point, Upper Canada (Ontario), where he and his father worked at a pig iron furnace and foundry. In 1834, Elijah established his own business in St. Thomas. As an American, Leonard had considerable trouble during the Rebellion of 1837, on several occasions being accused of spying. The depression of 1837 also proved to be a serious strain on the business.

Elijah Leonard, Jr.

For a short time Leonard considered returning to the United States. Instead, in 1838 he opened a machine shop and foundry in London. By then larger than St. Thomas, London had the attraction of being the district seat and a garrison town, with its attendant growth in business. By 1850, manufacturing boilers and steam engines had become the mainstay of his foundry. The company survived into the 1960s.

The railway construction boom of the early 1850s produced Leonard's first era of prosperity. He built rail cars and construction equipment for the Great Western and the London and Port Stanley railways. Unfortunately, these contracts proved so time-consuming that regular local business was lost. When railway construction disappeared in the 1857 depression, Leonard had little local business to fall back on. Prosperity did not return until the Civil War.

Mayor in 1857, Leonard built Locust Mount, now 661 Talbot Street, an imposing Regency style house, and lived there until his death in 1891.

Christopher Andreae

PAUL PEEL
(1860-1892)

In 1890, Paul Peel brought fame to London when he won a medal for his work *After The Bath* at the annual Paris Spring Salon. The international press wrote that the painting of the two nude children warming themselves before a glowing fire was the favourite. Sarah Bernhard vied with a rich American for the popular work. Ultimately, the Hungarian government carried off the prize for a rumoured $10,000. Today it remains a popular favourite at the Art Gallery of Ontario.

Paul received his early art training from his father, John Robert Peel, and art teacher William Lees Judson. Later, he attended the Pennsylvania Academy of Fine Art, working under the renowned American artist Thomas Eakins, from

Covent Garden Market, London, Ontario, 1883. Museum London, gift of Mrs Marjorie Barlow.

whom he acquired his technique for painting the nude. He then moved to Paris, where he studied with Benjamin Constant. Here he first won recognition at the Spring Salon of 1889 with an honourable mention for *The Modest Model* (purchased in 1990 by Museum London for $350,000).

In 1890, Paul returned to London, where his mother was dying. His return was marked by an exhibition and sale at the Tecumseh House Hotel of sixty-two canvasses that he had brought with him. None of the paintings sold. Bitterly disappointed, he left the city, never to return.

Ironically, when Paul died from pneumonia just two years later, the praise that had eluded him during his life poured forth upon his death. Overnight Canada had a new hero and there was an immediate clamour for his work.

Nancy Geddes Poole

ANNIE PIXLEY
(1855–1893)

Annie Pixley became a resident of London only posthumously, when she was buried in the striking mausoleum her husband and manager, Robert Fulford, had erected in Woodland Cemetery. An actress born in Brooklyn, New York, she appeared at least three times at the London Grand Opera House in the role for which she became famous, as the heroine of *M'liss, Child of the Sierras*, loosely based on a story by Bret Harte.

Enthusiastically reviewing her London debut in the role, the *London Free Press* of February 20, 1882, praised Pixley's portrayal of the "impulsive, high-spirited, clever and dashing" M'liss, which displayed "strong emotional power as well as a graceful and nimble manner." In 1886, while staying with relatives at Port Stanley, Pixley and Fulford's twelve-year-old son, Tommy, died in what was reportedly a drowning accident. In the intensity of her mourning, Annie lost her ebullience and her nimble grace, and she died a premature death in 1893.

Annie Pixley in her role as M'Liss, Child of the Sierras, c. 1885.

Designed by the architectural firm of Moore and Henry, the granite Pixley Mausoleum, which now holds the ashes of Tommy, Annie, and Robert, is appropriately theatrical. Ornate solid bronze gates provide a transparent curtain through which one can view the richly decorated interior, which holds a marble bust of Tommy and the reliquaries with his parents' remains. Solemn stone lions guard the entranceway, and, above the facade, expressive figures of Drama, Victory, and Music simultaneously recall the triumph of Annie's successes and the sorrow of her death.

Nancy Z. Tausky

Crystal Palace Exhibition Building, designed by William Robinson, Western Fair Grounds, 1872.

WILLIAM ROBINSON
(1812-1894)

As an architect, surveyor, and city engineer, William Robinson had a profound effect on London's physical development during its first quarter-century as a city. He first came to London in 1839 as a labourer, but a map he drew in 1840–41 shows loftier ambitions: on its margin is a small self-portrait of Robinson as a surveyor, leaning with his tools and map over a globe of the world. He moved to Toronto in 1842 for the training he needed. In 1857 he established his own practice in London, where he trained several of London's most influential architects, including three men who were to become future partners in his long-lived firm: Thomas Henry Tracy, George F. Durand, and John M. Moore. He also served as city engineer for twenty-one years while maintaining his private practice.

Robinson designed many of the city's early public and institutional buildings, including the Hellmuth Boys College, the Customs House, and St. Peter's Rectory (originally the Bishop's Palace). Among the still-standing buildings he designed are Christ Church, the Crystal Block on the northwest corner of Richmond and Dundas streets, First-St. Andrew's United Church and Manse, the Nathaniel Reid Cottage at 477 Waterloo Street, and the older pump house in Springbank Park. He was also the architect of London's first waterworks system, which, according to a speech by Alderman James Egan at Robinson's retirement banquet, he and Robinson developed with exemplary dedication: "If we had been married, the probability is that we would not have succeeded so well . . . . We were wedded to the scheme."

Nancy Z. Tausky

Anderson House, northeast corner, Dundas and Adelaide Streets, 1862.

MURRAY ANDERSON
(1814-1898)

An energetic and successful businessman, railway promoter, and politician, Murray Anderson was born on a farm near Niagara Falls, Upper Canada. After apprenticing as a tinsmith in Hamilton, he married Jane Kerr in 1838. In 1840, the family moved to London. Anderson was engaged in the fur trade, buying furs from Native Americans and selling them in New York. He also established a tin, stove, and foundry business, which became one of the largest in the city.

Captivated by the 1850s "railway fever," Anderson bought shares in the Great Western Railway (now the CN line) and persuaded the town to purchase stock as well. In 1853, the GWR was the first railway to reach London. He became the first mayor of the incorporated city of London in 1855.

His company, on the northwest corner of Richmond and Fullarton streets, manufactured stoves, stove pipe, tinware, washing machines, straw cutters, kettles, ploughs, cultivators and other implements. In 1856, a horrendous explosion at the foundry destroyed the establishment and killed five men. Anderson relocated the business to the southwest corner of Dundas and Adelaide streets where police headquarters stands today.

Anderson's decision to build his new plant on the outskirts of London provided the impetus for the development of London East as a place to live and work.

Glen Curnoe

BISHOP JOHN WALSH
(1830-1898)

John Walsh came to Canada from Ireland in 1852 and was ordained in Toronto in 1854, where he proved to be a fine priest, teacher, and administrator. He soon became a close collaborator with his bishop and was later recommended to be the bishop of the still-young Diocese of London, covering nine counties in southwestern Ontario. Inheriting a diocese with few churches and fewer priests, a large debt and a growing population, he set about the task of building up the diocese, while establishing strong relations with the broader community of London and with influential political friends, including Sir John A. Macdonald.

Seen as a leader among Catholics and in the community at large, Walsh worked tirelessly to promote Catholics for posts at all levels of government,

Bishop Walsh cradles the cathedral on his knee: a stained glass window from the sanctuary of St. Peter's Basilica.

convinced that his co-religionists should serve in public life. His crowning achievement in London was the construction of the new St. Peter's Cathedral. Such was the universal admiration felt for him that when funds dried up and he was unable to finish the towers, leading Protestants contacted Walsh and offered to pay for one tower if he could find funds for the other. By the time of his departure in 1889 he had built a financially sound and well-organized diocese with a growing Catholic population secure in its faith and position in secular society. He died July 31, 1898.

John P. Comiskey

BISHOP ISAAC HELLMUTH
(1817-1901)

Born into a rabbinical family, Isaac Hellmuth attended university at Breslau (now Wroclaw, Poland). Here he fell under the influence of a Christian missionary and decided to convert. This caused such a painful break with his family that for the rest of his life he used his mother's maiden name. He came to Canada in 1844. Trained at Bishop's University in Lennoxville, Quebec, he quickly became involved in evangelical church and university circles. After an argument, he left Bishop's and returned to England, where he became active in the Colonial Church and School Society. By 1856, he had returned to Canada as the Society's general superintendent there.

Hellmuth Girls' School, c.1910.

Hellmuth met Benjamin Cronyn about this time and by 1861 was persuaded to come to London as diocesan archdeacon. He was instrumental in raising funds for the proposed Huron College and became its first principal. Hellmuth was elected the second bishop of Huron in 1871. As bishop, Hellmuth planned a grand complex, the Cathedral of the Holy Trinity, to be located on lands south of Oxford Street between Richmond and Waterloo. Only the chapterhouse was ever completed; it was demolished to make way for the current Selby building's parking lot.

Hellmuth's most lasting accomplishment was the establishment of Western University (now the University of Western Ontario) in 1878. He was its first chancellor and its major financial supporter. His subsequent career in England was a quiet one, consisting mostly of a series of parish ministries until his retirement in 1899.

Douglas Leighton

RICHARD MAURICE BUCKE
(1837-1902)

Richard M. Bucke

Richard Bucke was a medical doctor, but it was his mystical experience of one poet's work that ultimately shaped his life.

Richard Maurice Bucke spent his childhood in London. After leaving home at 16, he travelled widely in the U.S. before entering McGill Medical School, where he graduated in 1862. He began his practice in Sarnia in 1865 and married Jessie Gurd the same year. In 1867 he first learned of Walt Whitman and his *Leaves of Grass*. In 1872, Richard had a profound mystical experience after an evening of reading Whitman. He left his practice in Sarnia in 1877 and became the superintendent of the Asylum for the Insane, first in Hamilton and then in London, where he spent the rest of his life. He also visited Whitman in 1877, an encounter that only heightened his idolatrous relationship with the poet. Whitman came to London in 1880 and stayed with Bucke, much to Jessie's dismay. They spent all their time working on a hagiographic biography of Whitman.

Whitman's influence, along with his own mystical experience, led Bucke to write *Cosmic Consciousness*. The book describes individuals who had had a mystical experience and the effect it had on their lives.

Bucke was also one of the founders of the Western Medical School. He died in 1902 after falling from his front porch.

Peter Rechnitzer

JANE KAY DARCH
(1834-1903)

Jane Darch

Jane Darch was a schoolteacher who became that Victorian rarity, a successful and visionary woman entrepreneur. After marrying into a London family of established saddlers and harness makers, she became the leading force behind the expansion of their enterprise. Seeing the potential of the market neighbourhood, she bought land and located the family business on Talbot Street opposite the Covent Garden Market before the mid-1850s. After her husband's premature death in 1867, she became the official head of the saddlery, as well as an influential voice in London's temperance movement. In 1877, she hired London's leading architect, William Robinson, to design a shop and residence at 377-379 Talbot Street. Under her leadership the family business so prospered that by 1903 the Darches built London's first "skyscraper" directly north of their Talbot Street premises; at a height of six storeys, the harness and trunk factory was then London's tallest building.

Jane died in 1903, just before the skyscraper reached its ambitious height, though her sons, William F. and J. Kay, carried on the business after her death. Her obituary spoke eloquently of both her character and her talent: "She was possessed of extraordinary business ability and integrity and by her carefulness and astuteness she built up what is probably the largest harness business in the West."

Nancy Z. Tausky

DR. CHARLES AUGUSTUS SIPPI
(1844-1906)

Charles A. Sippi, c. 1900.

Dr. Charles Sippi gave up one set of instruments for another. The son of a bandleader, he trained as a doctor in his native Ireland and arrived in Canada in 1865 to practise medicine in Port Stanley. Two years later, he was hired as house surgeon and teacher at London's Hellmuth College. But his love of music soon won out, and in 1874 he resigned to manage A. & S. Nordheimer's music store, at the corner of Dundas and Clarence streets. He was at the heart of the music scene in Victorian London. Sippi's diaries display an avidly social man, often out four or more nights each week to concerts, plays, and other entertainments. He was the longtime organist and choirmaster at Cronyn Memorial Church, just as his brother George fulfilled these duties at St. Paul's Cathedral. Charles co-founded the Ontario

Music Teachers' Association to encourage and improve the teaching of music in all its forms and was its first president. When he became bursar of the Asylum for the Insane in 1887, it soon gained renown for its band, drama club, and sporting day.

Charles Sippi's other great love was Ireland. He was one of the founders and first presidents of London's branch of the Irish Benevolent Society, working to unite Irish people of all faiths and to aid Irish immigrants. He mixed his two loves whenever possible. An obituary recalled that, "no programme was filled until the name of Dr. Sippi was put down for an Irish song."

Alan MacEachern

Hunt's City Mills, c. 1910.

EMMA BREWER HUNT
(c. 1822-1909)

Emma Brewer Hunt's life might have been far too busy for diary writing, but her husband, the merchant miller, builder, oil developer, and grocer, Charles Hunt, did keep a diary, and her life can be imagined through his voice.

Charles first saw Emma when he was an apprentice grocer on an errand in Cranborne, Dorsetshire, and she and her sisters were riding home from school on their pony. They next met in St. Thomas, Canada West, and married there in 1845. Charles's ambition to build a merchant flour mill took them to London in 1856. They bought a house off Ridout Street, overlooking both the Thames and the site of Hunt's City Mills. A footbridge connected the two properties.

Emma's life was full with children, their health, and schooling. In all they had eight children, and adopted two when Charles's brother William was kicked to death by a horse. They relished sleighing and skating on the rink that Charles built on Ridout Street. Charles was on the decorating committee when the Prince of Wales visited London in 1860. He and Emma attended the Ball and were presented to the future King Edward VII. They were also devoted parishioners at St. Paul's Cathedral.

In spite of pleurisy (treated with old whiskey and beef tea), rheumatism, and bad teeth (she had them all out and got a new set for $110), Emma lived to a ripe old age. Not so Charles, who died at age 51 in 1871.

Hilary Bates Neary

SIR JOHN CARLING
(1828–1911)

John Carling started as the head of a successful brewery but found his real calling in politics.

His father, Thomas Carling, a successful farmer in London Township, relocated to London in 1840 with his wife Margaret, to provide their three sons the opportunity of higher education. Using his father's Yorkshire recipe, he opened a brewery. In 1849, John and his brother William bought the brewery from their father. That same year, John married Hannah Dalton. On their honeymoon, they travelled the corduroy road to Port Stanley and took a steamer to Buffalo where they stayed a few days before returning to London by stage coach. In 1879, William died as a result of a disastrous fire which destroyed the brewery. It was quickly rebuilt.

Sir John Carling in court dress, c. 1893.

John Carling's distinguished political career began when he was elected a school trustee in 1850. He proceeded to win campaigns at every level of government, often using beer from the brewery to help swing votes his way. He became a member of Sir John A. Macdonald's cabinet and, as Minister of Agriculture, 1885–92, he founded the network of Dominion Experimental Farms. He was knighted by Queen Victoria in 1893.

Carling's political acumen benefited London in many ways. He was instrumental in moving the asylum here (now Regional Mental Health London), and establishing an infantry school (Wolseley Barracks). He arranged for three Crimean War (1854–56) cannons to be brought to London. They were later mounted in Victoria Park, which he helped to create.

In 1936, Carling's merged with the Kuntz Brewery of Waterloo and the London plant was closed. The Carling name, of course, is still famous in brewing circles.

Glen Curnoe

SENATOR THOMAS COFFEY
(1843-1914)

Senator Thomas Coffey

Surmounted by the most ornate and tallest Celtic cross in St. Peter's Cemetery the remains of five generations of the Coffey family lie, including Thomas Coffey.

The family emigrated from County Tipperary, Ireland, and arrived in London in 1856. Here, young Tom started out as a junior apprentice at the *London Prototype*. Later, he worked as a journeyman for the *London Free Press*. He became one of the printers at the *London Advertiser* when it was founded in 1863. Over the next 16 years, except for a brief stint as a grocer, he rose to become superintendent of the *Advertiser's* mechanical department. In 1879, Coffey purchased the bankrupt *Catholic Record*. Until his death, he was its owner and editor. This London weekly became "the premier Catholic weekly of its day" and, by 1913, had a circulation of almost 30,000.

While Coffey kept the *Record* politically independent but "fiercely Catholic," he himself was staunchly Liberal and never passed up an opportunity to trumpet the genius of Sir Wilfrid Laurier. Consequently, in 1903, Coffey was appointed to the Senate. A member of the Catholic Mutual Benefit Association for 38 years, he supported other Catholic fraternal organizations and was an ardent proponent of home rule for Ireland. In 1907, he was awarded an honorary LL.D. from the University of Ottawa for his contribution to Catholic journalism.

Dan Brock

THOMAS FRAZER KINGSMILL
(1840-1915)

In his lifetime, Thomas Frazer Kingsmill crossed the Atlantic more than 140 times, travelling frequently to suppliers' factories and mills in England and Europe to buy table linens, woollens and other textiles to supply his London store with the latest in stylish, quality goods.

Kingsmill's father opened a dry goods business in the 1830s in County Tipperary, Ireland, but it failed, a casualty of economic hardship, epidemic, and famine. Thomas Frazer Kingsmill left school and apprenticed himself to another dry goods merchant. In 1858, he and his wife, Annie, emigrated to

Thomas Frazer Kingsmill (at left in doorway) in front
of his carpet warehouse, Carling Street, 1897.

the United States, but the poor import trade resulting from the American Civil War forced them to move again in 1863 to Toronto, where Kingsmill found employment with W.A. Murray & Co. Two years later he became manager of Murray's London branch. When Kingsmill began his own business in 1865 at 130 Dundas Street, he advertised heavily in the local papers and introduced a one-price policy, to the relief of shoppers weary of the barter system.

In 1875, he acquired the adjoining property and built the store through to Carling Street. A carpet warehouse was added in 1884. In its early years, Kingsmill's specialized in cashmeres, embroidered handkerchiefs, gloves, carpets, and linens. Its product range was later expanded to include china, furniture, housewares, and lamps. The store expanded again in 1904.

Today, a member of the fifth generation of the family operates the store, now in its third successive building on the original site, the oldest retail business in London still owned by its founding family.

Arthur McClelland

JOSEPH DANBY SAUNBY
(c. 1837-1915)

Few businessmen successfully sue governments. Joseph Saunby took the City of London to court in 1897 and won, but the ordeal exhausted him.

In 1877, Saunby owned two successful merchant mills on the Thames, the North Branch Flouring Mill on Beaufort Street and the Blackfriar's Mill below Ridout Street. He was active in his community, a founder of Empress Avenue Methodist (now United) Church, and a member of London's Board of Trade. In 1878, the city of London developed its waterworks in

Saunby's mill, c. 1870.

Springbank and built a dam across the Thames to power the pumps. When water was low, flashboards were added to raise the dam's height. When four feet of flashboards were added, the water level rose upstream as far as the Blackfriar's Mill tailrace and interfered with Saunby's mill wheel. Frustrated, he brought a writ against the City of London Water Commissioners in 1897. The case went to the Ontario Trial Court in April 1902, and was decided in Saunby's favour. The city then took the case to the Ontario Court of Appeal, which upheld the lower court decision in 1903. Undaunted, the city then appealed to the Supreme Court of Canada, which allowed the appeal in 1904. Saunby was not intimidated; he appealed to the Privy Council in England. In 1905, this court confirmed the judgement of the Ontario courts, awarding Saunby costs and six years retroactive damages. He retired from the milling business soon after, and died in 1915. His mills are gone, but his name survives on nearby Saunby Street.

Hilary Bates Neary

WILLIAM NORMAN ASHPLANT
(1877-1916)

A true son of the British Empire, William Ashplant was born in Suffolk, trained as a surveyor, and took an apprenticeship in Cape Town that was soon interrupted by artillery service during the Boer War. Afterwards, his rise as an imperial civil servant was steady, taking him to ever more prestigious positions in South Africa, the Bahamas, and South Nigeria.

In 1913, he became City Engineer in London, Ontario, where his brother Henry was a prominent businessman. William shared Henry's house, joined a London militia regiment, and looked forward to a long career.

Major William N. Ashplant, 1st Battalion, c. 1915.

In 1914, war intervened. Canada's new army needed men with military experience, and Ashplant joined the 18th Battalion, Canadian Expeditionary Force, transferring to London's 33rd Battalion to help train new recruits. But officer casualties overseas were heavy, and in August 1916 he joined the 1st Battalion, then mired in the last stages of the long, bloody campaign on the Somme. On September 2, Ashplant was wounded in the head by a shellburst; he was back with the unit just eight days later.

On September 22, the 1st Battalion was thrown into the inferno again. This time, Major Ashplant was not among the survivors. The fate of this gallant Londoner is recorded laconically in his military file: "Was last seen by L/Cpl Hynds . . . in a shell hole with Machine Gun wounds in stomach and leg. This was on the night of Sept 22nd during the taking of trenches East of Courcelette. A search party on the morning of Sept 23rd failed to locate him." His body was never found.

Jonathan Vance

JOHN BAMLET SMALLMAN
(1849-1916)

He was called "Bam" by family and friends, and a "Merchant Prince of London" by fellow citizens. An immigrant from Ireland, Smallman opened his own dry goods store with a partner, Lemuel Hall Ingram, in 1877. Smallman & Ingram pioneered advanced retailing practices such as cash sales, refund or exchange, monthly stock replacement, and tight control of inventory.

After Ingram's death in 1901, Smallman took over the partnership and changed direction. He incorporated the business as a department store and expanded to 96,000 square feet of retail space with 42 departments, a restaurant, soda fountain, public washrooms, mail order service, and 200 employees. Smallman was liked and respected by his workers, many of whom were life-long employees. He encouraged them to buy company shares, reduced their hours of labour, and provided "modern" working conditions. His family motto was well earned: "My word is my bond."

Smallman played a low-key role in London affairs. Socially he was retiring but very interested in fine art, music, and literature. He supported the

The John B. Smallman mansion, now the Mocha Shriners headquarters, 468 Colborne Street.

Children's Aid Society and the Irish Benevolent Society. Although he remained a bachelor, living with his two stepsisters, he built one of London's finest homes in 1902. Its design shows his appreciation of fine workmanship and detail, such as egg and dart decoration on window frames, beautiful wood panelling throughout, fireplaces, and stained glass. His store, now Market Tower, still stands at Dundas and Richmond streets and his house on Colborne Street is now home to the Shriners.

Anne McKillop

SHADRACH Q. MARTIN
(1833–1917)

Shadrach Martin, known as "Shack," was born in Nashville, Tennessee, to African-American parents. He said his father was a free man, and that his mother was a slave, whose freedom had been purchased by her future husband.

At age 11 he was working on a steamboat as a cabin boy. At age thirteen he apprenticed in Memphis as a barber, then moved to Cincinnati where he stayed until 1854 when he moved to London. At that time, a shave cost six cents and a haircut cost twelve cents.

In the depression of the late 1850s, Shack returned to the U.S. where he obtained work as a barber on a Mississippi steamboat. At the beginning of

George Taylor's barber shop, London, c. 1908. Left to right: George Taylor, Shack Martin, and Thomas Logan.

the American Civil War, he was encouraged by one of his regular customers, a Union gunboat captain, to enlist in the navy. He was accepted and served for two years on the captain's gunboat. Receiving his honourable discharge in May, 1863, he returned to London.

Initially he worked in the barber shop at the Tecumseh House Hotel. Later he worked at various shops in central London until about age 80. Included among his customers were prominent Londoners: Sir John Carling, John Labatt, Elijah Leonard Jr., and Major Hume Cronyn.

On December 17, 1917, at eighty-four, in frail health and against family wishes, he insisted on going to the polls to vote for "Little Hume" (Major Hume Cronyn) who proceeded to win a seat in the federal election. The day after the election, Shack became acutely ill and died a few days later.

Glen Curnoe

HARRIET ANN BOOMER
(1835-1921)

Often called a pushy, nosy "old busybody," Harriet Boomer was strong-willed and forceful in expressing her opinions, an assertiveness considered unwomanly in many circles.

She grew up in Somerset, England, and married a businessman, Alfred Roche, who died as they were sailing home to England from South Africa. Her book, *On Trek in the Transvaal*, still makes interesting reading.

She came to London in 1878 with her second husband, Reverend Michael Boomer, first provost of the Western University. Mrs Boomer gave her new city and its institutions indefatigable energy and service, becoming an inspiration for women who worked to improve the lot of their families. As

Harriet Boomer

president of the London Council of Women, she supported the formation of a local branch of the Victorian Order of Nurses. She raised funds for the children's wing of Victoria Hospital and established the first Red Cross Society to help soldiers in the Boer War. In the First World War the society raised almost half a million dollars. Her lobbying for more technical education and home economics classes contributed to the London Board of Education's decision to build what would become Beal Technical School. She became the board's first female trustee in 1898. A local chapter of the IODE was named after her.

On her death in 1921, the *Free Press* called her "London's most philanthropic and patriotic worker." She is recognized on the *People and the City* monument on Wellington Street and by a plaque at H.B. Beal Secondary School.

Barbara Baker Graham

DR. CLARENCE THOMAS CAMPBELL
(1843-1922)

Clarence Campbell, c. 1905.

Dr. Clarence Campbell enjoyed three careers, and contributed much through his passions, his politics, and his practice.

Dr. Cl.T. Campbell, as he was known locally, was born in London to a Scots-Irish father and a West Indian mother. He studied medicine with the American Quaker and homeopath, Dr. Joseph J. Lancaster, and then at the Cleveland Western Medical College and the Homeopathic College of Philadelphia. His practice included caring for patients in charitable institutions, serving on Ontario and Canadian Medical Councils, and lobbying for keeping London's new Victoria Hospital within easy reach of the poor.

He also gave time and energy to civic affairs, serving as alderman, mayor in 1905, chairman of the Board of Education in 1884, and London District Post Office Inspector between 1906 and 1912. He was also a member of the Free Masons (Royal Arcanum), the Independent Order of Foresters, and St. Paul's Cathedral.

Campbell's third career was as a historian. He put his extensive knowledge of London's past to good use as a speaker and writer, publishing *Pioneer Days in London* in 1921. He became the London and Middlesex Historical Society's first president in 1901. Like Dr. Edwin Seaborn, who revived the Society in the 1930s, Campbell combined his passions for medicine and local history.

Post Office Inspector Clarence Campbell in his office.

When his funeral cortege left 327 Queens Avenue, it was joined by officials of the city and the Foresters, paying him respectful tribute. The Library Board praised him as "a worthy citizen and a good friend" who had enriched London's life with remarkable gifts. Campbell left no descendants, but students of London's past acknowledge his rich historical legacy.

Elizabeth Spicer

CHARLES HENRY IVEY
(1856-1922)

Charles Henry and Louise Green Ivey founded one of the most successful and philanthropic families in London. Ivey was born in Jarvis, Haldimand County, into a farming family that had emigrated from Cornwall in 1841.

Deciding on a legal career, he attended Victoria College in Cobourg, where he obtained his B.A. in 1880 and afterwards articled with London firms. In 1885, he married Louise Green of London.

He began practising law in 1883 and five years later formed a partnership with Isidore F. Hellmuth, a son of Anglican Bishop Isaac Hellmuth. The business flourished, with Hellmuth's interests lying in court work and Ivey's in commercial law.

When the local owners of the London Street Railway were unable to afford electrification in 1893, Cleveland-based clients of Hellmuth & Ivey purchased the business which Ivey afterwards supervised.

Hellmuth moved to Toronto in 1900, and Ivey continued the London business, which he developed into one of the major legal firms in the city, with many business accounts and connections in Montreal and the United States. He successfully appealed one case to the Judicial Committee of the Privy Council in London, England. (See Joseph Danby Saunby.)

Among his clients was the Empire Brass Company (EMCO) which he incorporated in 1905, becoming a stockholder. His older son, Charles Herbert Ivey, continued this association. The legal business was carried on by his younger son, Richard G. Ivey.

Charles Ivey was an active member of the First Methodist (now Metropolitan United) Church and was involved in charitable activities.

Frederick H. Armstrong

ELLEN H. GREGSTEN
(1831-1923)

An Irish orphan, Ellen was raised in Liverpool by her brother. She married William Gregsten, a dry goods merchant, and moved to London in 1860. She began charitable work at North Street Methodist Church teaching a Sunday school class called "The Busy Bees." Her students called her "Mother Bee," and later, "Queen Bee."

In 1874–75 the Women's Christian Association was established for the care of the poor and the sick. Under Gregsten's presidency, the WCA launched a soup kitchen for the unemployed at Covent Garden Market.

Next they opened the Women's Refuge and Children's Home to provide destitute women with skills and moral and religious improvement so that they could keep their children. The WCA was advised by a committee of influential men, and retained doctors to provide free medical services for their clients. They opened a cottage for aged women, then one for old men, both of which were replaced in 1892 by a large brick building at Richmond

Ellen Gregsten

and Victoria streets donated by biscuit manufacturer Thomas McCormick. Today's McCormick Home and Alzheimer Outreach Centre will soon move to west London.

In 1887, the WCA launched the Queen Victoria Golden Jubilee Fund to build a hospital for "incurables." Today, Parkwood Hospital for rehabilitation and long-term care is the largest of its kind in western Ontario. Mrs Gregsten was also treasurer of the Protestant Orphans' Home, today the Merrymount Children's Centre. She lived to age 92 in her cozy Colborne Street cottage. Her faithful teaching and humble service endeared her to generations of Londoners.

Netta Brandon

THE LOMBARDO
ORCHESTRA
(1918-1923)

Music was one of the cornerstones of London's Italian community and its orchestras were considered exotic and fashionable at society functions. Guy Lombardo was born into this milieu in 1902, and four of his siblings followed

The Lombardo Orchestra at the Hopkins Casino in Port Stanley, 1923. From left to right: Archie Cunningham, Ernie Furanna, Carmen Lombardo, Lebert Lombardo, Eddie Masuret, George Gowans, Freddie Kreitzer, Francis "Muff" Henry and Guy Lombardo.

him into the big band business: Carmen, Lebert, Victor, and baby sister, Rose Marie.

From a modest duet for the Mother's Club (Carmen on flute, Guy on violin), the Lombardo Orchestra grew to include Lebert on trumpet and boyhood chum Freddie Kreitzer on piano. In the spring of 1918, they landed their first important gig when Ontario Hydro founder Sir Adam Beck hired the Lombardos to play at a party for his daughter. Over the next four years the band was kept busy at a variety of venues including the Springbank Pavillion and the Winter Garden dance hall.

In the summer of 1923, the Lombardo Orchestra was hired as the house band for the Hopkins Casino at the popular Lake Erie resort town of Port Stanley. The added exposure to American fans and headliners convinced the musicians they were ready to tackle the United States.

During the fall, Guy bluffed his way into a one-night stand at the Elk's Club in Cleveland, Ohio. In November, the Lombardo Band played its final set at the Winter Garden. A few hours later, ten young musicians boarded a train for Cleveland and an uncertain future. They would return the following May, a little more famous and sporting a new name: Guy Lombardo and His Royal Canadians.

Christopher Doty

ADAM BECK
(1857-1925)

In 1902, Sir Adam Beck, one of London's great public servants, won both the city's mayoral race and London's seat for the Conservatives in the provincial election. That same year, strikes in the U.S. coal fields stopped shipments to Ontario, which was entirely dependent on coal-fired plants for its electricity. Along with others, Beck saw a solution in the hydro power potential of Niagara Falls. He was soon head of an organization of municipalities that sought a way to protect Niagara's power from private monopolies and U.S. interests.

Adam Beck, c. 1910.

In 1906, the province created the Hydro-Electric Power Commission of Ontario to distribute and later generate power. Beck was named chairman, and held the office until his death. London's first public power arrived from Niagara in 1910, the year Beck established another public organization: the London Health Association. The LHA was formed to build a sanitorium in Byron for tuberculosis sufferers, who were then dying at a rate of 2,000 a year in Ontario. The LHA later built University Hospital in 1972.

A competitive horseman as a young man, Beck joined the London Hunt and Country Club, where he met many of London's leaders, and his future wife, Lillian Ottaway. They moved into Headley, a mansion on Richmond Street that has since been reconstructed near the original site.

When Beck died, the business of the city stopped as his funeral cortege made its way to the CNR station on York Street. From there his body was taken to Hamilton to be interred next to his wife.

Mike Baker

Adam Beck, equestrian, c. 1910.

CHIEF W.T.T. WILLIAMS
(1843-1927)

W.T.T. Williams, c. 1900.

William Thomas Trounce Williams' 43-year tenure as Chief Constable (1877–1920) was a record for the city and, perhaps, the nation.

After immigrating to Canada from England, Williams rose to prominence in the Toronto police force during the Pilgrimage Riots of 1876 when, at the head of 20 officers, he arrested rioters who had attacked Roman Catholic processions. He took over as London's chief a year later.

Williams' starting salary was $1,000 per year at a time when the annual operating cost of the London force was only $15,000, but he proved worthy of his wage. One of his many accomplishments was a new central police station at 140 Carling Street, in 1882. A year earlier, under Williams' guidance, the police had become one of the city's first telephone subscribers. In 1913, Williams introduced the force's first motorized vehicle, a paddy wagon, and after the First World War he helped ensure officers regained their rank and seniority when they returned from overseas.

Williams was known for his height and great physical strength; he made an arrest in his 70s. But in spite of a no-nonsense approach to policing and a somewhat puritanical streak, he had a reputation for being kind to people looking for advice. When Williams took over in 1877, London's police force was in disarray, but when he left in 1920 the department was "one of the most highly regarded in the Dominion."

Chief Williams retired to live with family in Portland, Oregon, where he died in 1927.

Mark Richardson

VICTORIA GRACE BLACKBURN
(1865-1928)

When Victoria Grace Blackburn died on March 4, 1928, she left an estate of $40,987.87. It was probably the last time anyone was able to assess her exact worth. Blackburn, the leading intellectual and power behind the throne of her family's London media dynasty, left a vast, uncollected ocean of words — 20, 50, perhaps 100 times 40,000 — far outnumbering the count of her dollars. Often writing under the name Fanfan, Blackburn was a novelist, poet, playwright, critic, world traveller, essayist, and theatre lover. For the last 10 years of her life, as assistant managing editor of the *London Free Press*, she was the embodiment of the powerful, pre-feminist ideal — able to combine her family's ownership of the newspaper with her own intellect and interests. In this, she had able allies in the flock of Blackburn sisters who lived with her at 652 Talbot Street. Born in Quebec City, she was educated in London and taught briefly in the United States. By early 1894, her first writing appeared. In 1900, she joined the staff of the *Free Press*, writing criticism, poetry — pretty much what she pleased, one suspects.

Title page,
The Man
Child, *1930.*

A novel, *The Man Child*, published two years after her death from cancer, is a vivid portrayal of a slightly fictionalized London during the years leading up to the First World War. It conveys the anguish on the home front — and in the trenches — once the conflict broke out. Her plays, including the satiric *The Little Gray*, are talky, intelligent, and self-confident.

Not unlike that Fanfan woman herself.

James Reaney

ANNIE LAURIE (CRIPPEN) AND WILLIAM JOHN ANTHISTLE

(1862-1937) AND (1854-1929) RESPECTIVELY

William Anthistle was born in London to Irish immigrants, John and Margaret Anthistle. They built a home at the southwest corner of Waterloo and Cheapside streets on property purchased from Richard Jones Evans in 1863. John was a lime burner at Evans' lime and gravel pit until his death in 1876. William bought some of Evans' land on Grosvenor, Wellington, and Cromwell streets, including the pit. After the gymnasium and roof of the Hellmuth Boys' College collapsed in 1878, William re-erected the structure in his pit, parged it with cement, and inscribed the date on its western end.

William married Annie Crippen in Southwold Township, Elgin County, in 1881. Although her family had lived there, near Fingal, she was born in Illinois. William, who had been a teamster, now became a lime burner like his father, and built his and Annie's home at 309 Cromwell Street overlooking the pit. Here they raised five children. After a neighbour, Ebenezer North, invented a secret process for making concrete tile, using gravel from Anthistle's pit, William developed his own method of manufacturing sewer pipes and tiles in the 1890s. He also laid many of London's earliest concrete sidewalks around 1900.

Anthistle house, 309 Cromwell Street.

William expanded his product line to include cement blocks and burial vaults. In the meantime, Annie had her own business, running a fancy goods shop downtown from 1902 to 1917. Following William's death in 1929, Annie continued his business across from their house. After she died in 1937, the city claimed the pit for tax arrears. It became Doidge Park in 1958.

Catherine B. McEwen

BISHOP MICHAEL FRANCIS FALLON
(1867-1931)

Michael Francis Fallon was an energetic and creative builder of the Roman Catholic Diocese of London. Though his episcopal motto was *Iustitia et Pax* (Justice and Peace), his achievements are often overshadowed by his role in a bitter national struggle over language rights. Born in Kingston, he became pastor of Holy Angels, Buffalo, in 1901 and in 1909 was named Bishop of London. In 1912, perhaps using funds supplied by Buffalo admirers, he acquired for $9,500 a gracious residence — Blackfriars — at 90 Central Avenue.

His achievements were many: new parishes, new schools, establishing St.

Peter's Seminary in 1912, and founding Brescia Hall as a college for girls. He supported Irish home rule and labour's right to collective bargaining. In 1910, he strongly criticized education standards in the bilingual schools of his diocese. This touched off a painful controversy with francophone groups that dragged on for many years. In 1912, the Ontario Department of Education issued Regulation 17 to entrench English as the language of instruction in Ontario schools. Endorsed by Fallon, this regulation stirred deep opposition among French Canadians. Fallon publicly supported the Union Government formed in 1917, which was an anathema to Quebec. Though a devout Catholic and a man of good works, he was also an Ontarian living in a troubled time and should be understood in this context.

Bishop Fallon

Fallon is buried in the crypt of St. Peter's Seminary. In his will, he affirmed his faith and begged the pardon of all whom he might have "offended or scandalized." Among his many benefactions was $10,000 to establish the "Fallon Chair of French Language and Literature" at St. Peter's Seminary.

Peter Neary

JAMES JENKINS
(1884-1931)

James F. Jenkins became part of a small African-Canadian community when he came to London in 1907 and joined its leading church, the Beth Emmanuel British Methodist Episcopal Church. Jenkins was born in Georgia and educated in Atlanta, where he may have come into contact with W.E.B. Dubois, a founder of the National Association for the Advancement of Colored People (NAACP), established in 1909. Dubois would also become the editor of the NAACP's magazine, *The Crisis*, which began publishing a year later.

In 1924, Jenkins formed the Canadian League for the Advancement of Coloured People. The League included both African-Canadian and white Londoners and was organized "to improve the condition of the coloured people of Canada," particularly by providing educational opportunities for the young, a response to a nationwide loss of talented, younger African-Canadian people to the United States.

The League had an official newspaper, *The Dawn of Tomorrow*, which Jenkins had founded in 1923. *The Dawn* was to serve many purposes. It informed the African-Canadian community on issues of the day, and it would bring African-Canadian communities in other Ontario towns and cities closer together by listing their activities in columns of social and church notices.

The death of editor James Jenkins is announced on the front page of the May 18, 1931, edition of The Dawn of Tomorrow.

James Jenkins died suddenly following surgery in 1931. His widow, Christina, continued to put out the paper with the help of her large family. At its height, about 1971, it had a total circulation of 48,000, and 21,000 subscribers in various parts of the world. It is still published today, with issues appearing at Easter and Christmas.

Mike Baker

JOE MARKS
(1858-1932)

Late Victorian Canada saw great industrial progress but also great industrial turmoil. The Philadelphia-based Knights of Labor targeted London for their activities. Among their enthusiastic recruits was a young tinsmith on the Great Western Railway named Joseph Marks. Marks was a founder of the London District Trades and Labour Council and of the Industrial Brotherhood in 1891.

After a portrait in the Templar Quarterly, *1886.*

The following year he launched the *Industrial Banner*, a monthly broadsheet devoted to union causes. Marks was always interested in educating the working class and leading unionists and encouraged them to enter into political fields. He opened the United Labour Hall at 465–467 Dufferin Avenue so that issues critical to labour could be discussed. In 1896, Marks and four colleagues ran for city council. None was elected, but three years later, unionist Frank Plant won a seat. In 1906, Marks managed a provincial by-election for Allen Studholme, who won a seat for the Independent Labour Party (ILP) in Hamilton.

In 1912, Marks moved to Toronto, where he remained active in radical politics. In 1919, twelve ILP candidates were elected to the Ontario Legislature. They joined with a larger group of members elected by the United Farmers of Ontario to form the government. Marks, now a government supporter, was elected secretary of the ILP.

At his death in November 1932, Marks was laid to rest in London's Mount Pleasant Cemetery. His grave for many years was the site of Labour Day celebrations.

David Spencer

ELSIE PERRIN WILLIAMS
(1878?-1934)

Elsie Perrin Williams was the only child of nationally renowned biscuit and candy manufacturer, Daniel Simmons Perrin, and was reared in considerable comfort, including stays at Windermere, the family's summer home overlooking the Medway Valley. When she married Dr. Hadley Williams in 1905, they made Windermere their permanent home. Elsie was left a sizable inheritance from her father's estate and in 1916 replaced the original home with a Spanish Colonial Revival house. An accomplished artist and member of the Women's Art Club, Elsie helped design the new Windermere. (She designed its much earlier gatehouse when she was only 15.) She was also a golf enthusiast, and enjoyed the sport both on her nine-hole course at the

Elsie Perrin Williams in Venice.

estate, and on greens around the world.

When Hadley died in 1932, Elsie made major revisions to her will. She left Windermere and the surrounding parkland to the city of London, with an endowment of over one million dollars to maintain the property. The city, however, needed funds for capital projects immediately and sought to break the will. In 1938, the Province enacted legislation giving the city access to the endowment with which a new wing of the former Victoria Hospital (now the South Street campus of the London Health Sciences Centre) and a new art gallery and library at 305 Queens Avenue (now closed) were built.

The house was occupied by Elsie's housekeeper, Harriet Corbett, until she died in 1979. Since then the Heritage London Foundation has operated a reception centre at the estate and the grounds have been maintained as a public park.

Leith Peterson

SAMUEL BAKER
(1860-1936)

*Sam Baker,
c. 1915.*

Sam Baker's love of history led to his much praised and still useful 1924 booklet, *The Rise and Progress of London.* "I love London, a city of homes, a metropolitan and university community, with happy, contented and industrious people," wrote Baker, London's feisty city clerk for more than 29 years. He had been principal of the Wesleyan School in Blaenavon, Wales, and also English featherweight boxing champion before immigrating in 1886 with his wife, Mary Vaughan. In Canada, he hoped to prove himself where he could not in Britain's class-ridden society. Baker taught in Westminster Township, later becoming principal of St. George's School in London.

A passion for municipal government led Sam to became London's city clerk in 1904. This role earned him both respect and power. Politicians came and went, but Sam remained, with an ever-growing knowledge of civic government. He wrote for municipal journals, gave speeches on municipal government across Canada, and was admired for his humour and knowledge.

Local journalists told many Baker stories, not all complimentary, but always amusing. An individualist with a fiery temper and a passion for fairness and equality, he referred to his boxing prowess whenever necessary. There were even rumours of physical fights in London's Council Chambers. Baker was proud of these myths. He revelled in committee meetings, attending over 180 to plan London's Centennial in 1926.

Baker sacrificed much family life in his commitment to civic responsibilities. He later regretted this neglect, but he served the city with his whole heart.

Barbara Baker Graham

WILLIAM EDWIN SAUNDERS
(1861-1943)

Dr. W.E. Saunders was an internationally known naturalist, one of four brothers renowned for scientific endeavour. His brother, Charles, was knighted for developing Marquis Wheat. Saunders Secondary School in London was named for this scientific family.

A North American expert in the field of ornithology (study of birds), William Saunders possibly contributed more than anyone else to the preservation and study of our natural world.

He was a pharmacologist, and taught practical chemistry at the London Medical School, but he was also a naturalist, librarian, parks commissioner, author, and businessman. Saunders was passionate about the time he spent in the outdoors, writing hundreds of articles on nature and collecting thousands

The Saunders brothers, 1907. Left to right, top: Charles and Henry; bottom: Percy, William, and Fred.

of wildlife specimens for advanced research. He was a founder of the Ontario Entomological Society (insects), and member of the American Society of Mammalogists, the American Ornithologists Union, and the American Peony Society.

The Federation of Ontario Naturalists recognized his expertise, leadership, and devotion to wildlife by making him its first president in 1931. Saunders served in that capacity until his death. He was instrumental in preserving what eventually became Point Pelee National Park on the north shore of Lake Erie, and Westminster Ponds in London.

From 1929 to 1943, Saunders wrote the "Nature Week by Week" column in the *London Free Press*. He was a founding member of the London Horticultural Society, the London & Middlesex Historical Society, and the McIllwraith Field Naturalist Society. The University of Western Ontario honoured him with a Doctor of Laws degree in 1936.

Cliff Oliver

ARTHUR STRINGER
(1874-1950)

In 1886, Arthur earned the highest standing in the entrance examinations to the London Collegiate Institute, where he later revealed his literary interests by founding a magazine, *Chips*.

It was the beginning of a creative career that would yield 15 volumes of poetry, 45 works of fiction, and several screenplays. Thirty of his stories were made into movies, his collection of poems, *Open Water* (1914), is considered a precursor of modern Canadian poetry, and his Prairie Trilogy of novels (1915–22) has been identified as an influence on the development of modern Canadian fiction.

In a brief and witty chronology of his life, Stringer emerges as adventurous, even rebellious, witty and self-deprecating; in 1884, he was "rescued from the . . . Thames after going down twice"; in 1886 he wrote "his first poem on [the] spare-room wall and was spanked for same"; in 1888, he "robbed [his] Aunt Agatha's orchard of [its] entire cherry crop"; and in 1893, the authorities at Wycliffe College, Toronto, "requested [he] try some other college, and [he] did so." He tried Oxford University, worked briefly for the *Montreal Herald*, then took his journalistic skills to New York, where he moved in bohemian circles that included Bliss Carman, Charles G.D. Roberts, and other expatriate Canadian writers.

After his first marriage ended in divorce, Stringer married his cousin, Margaret Arbuthnott, and spent a year in Hollywood writing screenplays. In

The boyhood home of Arthur Stringer, 64 Elmwood Avenue East.

1921, they moved to Mountain Lakes, New Jersey, their home base for extensive travels and camping expeditions and the final resting place of Arthur Stringer's restless spirit.

David M.R. Bentley

HENRY JAMES JONES
(1864–1952)

Henry James Jones created two of London's oldest family-owned enterprises, a business legacy stretching from 1882 to the present. Jones was seven years old when he arrived in London from England in 1872 with his family.

Early Jones Company lithographing plant, 1155 Dundas Street.

While working as a compositor on the *London Advertiser*, he joined up with Frank Lawson, a young reporter. They bought a small monthly paper, *The Family Circle*, and went into business together. Printing and lithographing proved to be more profitable than publishing, and eventually Lawson & Jones Limited was marketing its high-quality products from coast to coast.

In 1913, Jones sold his interest in the company to Ray Lawson and established both H.J. Jones Sons Limited, a printing and lithographing venture, and the London Paper Company, to supply the paper it required. Jones placed his three eldest sons in charge of the printing and paper companies, and in 1920 he established Jones Box and Label for his three younger sons to manage.

Although the London Paper Company is no longer operating, the other two businesses are still owned by Henry's descendants. H.J. Jones Sons Limited now produces high-quality printing in a factory at 1155 Dundas Street, on the site where Henry founded his original print shop in 1913. Jones Box and Label is now Jones Packaging, an international packaging supplier in a state-of-the-art plant that was built in 1999 near London Airport.

William Corfield

JOHN SACKVILLE LABATT
(1880-1952)

John Sackville Labatt, the millionaire London brewer, held the dubious distinction of being the victim of Canada's first publicized kidnapping for ransom. Until August 1934, kidnapping was considered a "typically American" crime. Then armed gunmen "snatched" Labatt as he returned to London from a Lake Huron cottage. The event turned into such a comedy of errors that people believed the abduction was an elaborate publicity stunt.

Labatt, a McGill University graduate, joined the family business at age 20. Upon his father's death in 1915, he became president of the company. As one of London's wealthiest residents, Labatt took a keen interest in the city's cultural and sporting life. A member of the London Hunt and Country Club and St. Paul's Cathedral, he served as a director of Beck Memorial Sanitorium. He also donated Tecumseh Park (renamed Labatt Memorial Park) to the city.

John S. Labatt

After forcing his car off the road, the kidnappers hid Labatt in a secluded Muskoka cottage, leaving behind a ransom note demanding $150,000 in cash. After three days, worried about Labatt's failing health and the growing police dragnet, the kidnappers released their victim in

Ransom note left in Labatt's car.

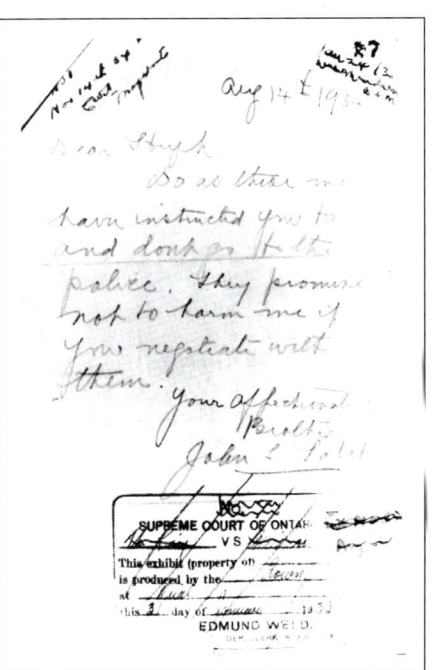

Letter John wrote to his brother Hugh warning him not to go to the police, 1934.

Toronto, courteously handing him cab fare. The gang's proceeds for their crime were $100.

After his release, Labatt had heavy plate glass installed in his office and avoided public places for the rest of his life. In 1952, the brewery executive died at his summer home in Port Stanley.

Alice M. Gibb

MISS KATE MATTHEWS
(1878-1955)

One of London's premier educators, Kate Matthews appreciated the individuality of each child and always strove for a personal connection with her students. Ever patient, respectful, and attentive, Matthews instilled in her pupils a vital confidence in their abilities. They responded with equal devotion, sending their own children to her school, and returning faithfully to school reunions.

Born in England in 1878, Kate Matthews immigrated to British Columbia in 1895. In 1912, she moved to London, where St. Paul's Anglican Cathedral became the focal point of her personal and public life.

Matthews always believed that London was well served by its public education system, but that there was a place for an alternative school in London. So, in 1918 she founded St. Paul's Private School in the basement of the cathedral, beginning with only six very young students. Miss Matthews School, now

Kate Matthews with two students, c. 1950.

Matthews Hall, grew to become London's most respected private school.

Kate Matthews remained headmistress of her school until 1950. She continued teaching until her retirement because she knew the best way to impart her approach to her teachers was by example.

Matthews was also much admired for her work in the church, and with the Guiding movement. She was so respected by her fellow Londoners that the University of Western Ontario recognized her remarkable achievements with an honorary Doctorate of Letters in 1950.

Miss Matthews' death in 1955 marked a mournful day for hundreds of children and adults who had been her students, as well as for countless people in the larger community who had been touched by her work and words.

Christian Hegele

JANET BARBARA GROSHOW
(1868-1960)

Most mothers whose sons fought in the First World War felt helpless when hearing they had been wounded or killed. Not so Janet Groshow. When her youngest son, William, was reported missing in action in April 1915, she left for France. Leaving her position as Matron of London's Victoria Home for Incurables (now Parkwood Hospital), Janet joined the Canadian Army Medical Corps (CAMC), hoping to discover his fate. Overseas, she served as

Janet Groshow and the other organizers of the 1938 Old Boys Reunion.

Matron at a Red Cross Hospital in Kent, as Superintendent of CAMC's Cliveden Hospital, on HM Transport 2810, which carried troops across the Atlantic, and at No. 7 Canadian General Hospital in Étaples, France.

In 1916 her two other sons, Thomas and James, joined the Canadian Expeditionary Force. William died at Ypres, and both Thomas and James were wounded in action. Janet was invalided out in 1919 with tuberculosis and returned to London to be restored to health at the Queen Alexandra Sanitorium. For the rest of her life she devoted herself first to the welfare of tuberculous veterans and their families and second to supporting active members of the forces. She was the first female president of a soldier's branch of the Canadian Legion of the British Empire Service League, Byron Branch 69 (Tubercular Veterans' Section), which eventually honoured her with life membership. During the Second World War, she provided hospitality to wounded soldiers and assisted war brides arriving in London. Her life exemplified London's strong connection to the British Empire and its military traditions.

Hilary Bates Neary

MARIAN KEITH [MARY ESTHER (MILLER) MACGREGOR]
(1874-1961)

London's claim to literary fame during the first half of the 20th century rested largely on the novels of Mary Esther MacGregor, who wrote under the pseudonym Marian Keith. She was the wife of Rev. Donald MacGregor, minister of London's St. Andrew's Presbyterian (now First-St. Andrew's United) Church, 1914 to 1936. Like her contemporary, Lucy Maud Montgomery, MacGregor juggled her busy public life as a minister's wife with the private demands of a writer. Seven of her 17 books were written at the manse on Queens Avenue. Her popular Sunday School club for girls, proudly named the Marian Keith Club by its denominationally diverse membership, taught an awareness of the social and missionary issues treated in her novels.

Mary Esther Miller's family were avid readers: "To me everything that could be asked of life dwelt within the covers of books," she later recalled. She published her first novel, *Duncan Polite* (1905), when teaching high school in Orillia. She married the Rev. MacGregor in 1909. Their ministry took them to many postings before they retired to a farm on Georgian Bay.

*Marian Keith at her desk,
and with her husband at
her home on Georgian Bay.*

Keith's writings advocate a trust in divine mercy and a social conscience that seeks to improve life for the poor and uneducated. Her novels achieve an even broader objective, portraying with wit, incisive sympathy, and a marked ability to evoke place, both the character of Ontario's early Scottish settlers and the tensions produced by societies in flux. Among other issues she depicts the difficulties of resolving conflicts between Scots and Irish, the effects of education and urbanization on farming societies, and the simultaneously enriching and impoverishing effects of industrialization on Ontario's small towns.

Hilary Bates Neary and Nancy Z. Tausky

WILLIAM RILEY STANSELL
(1881-1961)

Born in Courtland, Ontario, and apprenticed as a baker, William Stansell quickly moved into the sales of bakery equipment and then into the emerging automobile industry of Detroit. Briefly employed at Packard, he then became the manager of the Denby Truck Company's factory in Chatham,

William Stansell

Ontario where he began to lay the groundwork for the production of a mid-to-high-priced assembled automobile: the London Six. Stansell briefly considered Amherstburg on the Detroit River as a site to establish operations, but by 1921 he had set up shop in London.

London Motors Limited acquired space on Hale Street, just north of the rail line. The Stansell family lived nearby at 367 Hale Street. The firm acquired a second site consisting of several buildings between King and York streets, along the east side of Ridout Street. From 1921 to about 1924, 98 London Sixes were built at the King Street location, originally the site of the White Portable Steam Engine Company. "Canada's Quality Car" was expensive, ranging in price from $2700 to $3700, but it was powerful and technologically advanced. A natural publicist and salesman, Stansell scored his greatest coup in April of 1922 when Governor General Lord Byng and his party were transported to and from the ground-breaking ceremony for the new campus of Western University in a group of London Sixes.

The company collapsed in the uncertain times of the mid-1920s, leaving many local investors confused and angry. Stansell briefly sold real estate in London before leaving for Detroit around 1928. The factory site on King Street was demolished in 2004.

Douglas Leighton

A London Six in front of the factory on King Street, c. 1925.

RICHARD EDWIN CROUCH
(1894-1962)

Richard Crouch's studies in political economy at the Western University were interrupted by service with No. 10 Stationary Hospital at Calais, France, during the First World War. Before demobilizing, he attended the London School of Economics. Graduating from Western in 1920, he received a scholarship to study at the Universities of Dijon and Paris. Returning to London, Crouch lectured in Western's Extension Department and organized the Workers' Educational Association for Western Ontario.

Richard E. Crouch

Crouch succeeded Dr. Fred Landon as chief librarian at the London Public Library in 1923. He inherited an 1895 library building at Queens and Wellington streets that was inadequate and overcrowded. An opportunity to replace it finally appeared in 1934, when biscuit heiress Elsie Perrin Williams left her estate to the city, along with a sizable endowment. In 1940, a new library, art gallery, and museum bearing Elsie's name opened at 305 Queens Avenue. Here Crouch realized his vision of the library as community centre fostering culture and adult education, with art gallery, film, and music departments interwoven with traditional library service.

Crouch founded the London Council for Adult Education in 1945, and was active in the pioneering radio work of the Canadian Association for Adult Education. Library employees remember him as a progressive administrator who encouraged them to unionize for improved working conditions. In 1958, a new library on Hamilton Road was named the Richard E. Crouch Branch Library.

This man of talents and vision retired in April 1961 after serving 38 years as London's chief librarian.

Arthur McClelland

IVAN H. SMITH,
MD, MSC, FRCS
(1904-1962)

Years of scientific probing into the secrets of the atom eventually led to the atomic bomb and the end of the Second World War. Soon after, at the University of Saskatchewan and at the Chalk River plant, physicist Harold Johns began the development of a machine, the so-called cobalt bomb, using radioactive cobalt-60 to fight the war on cancer.

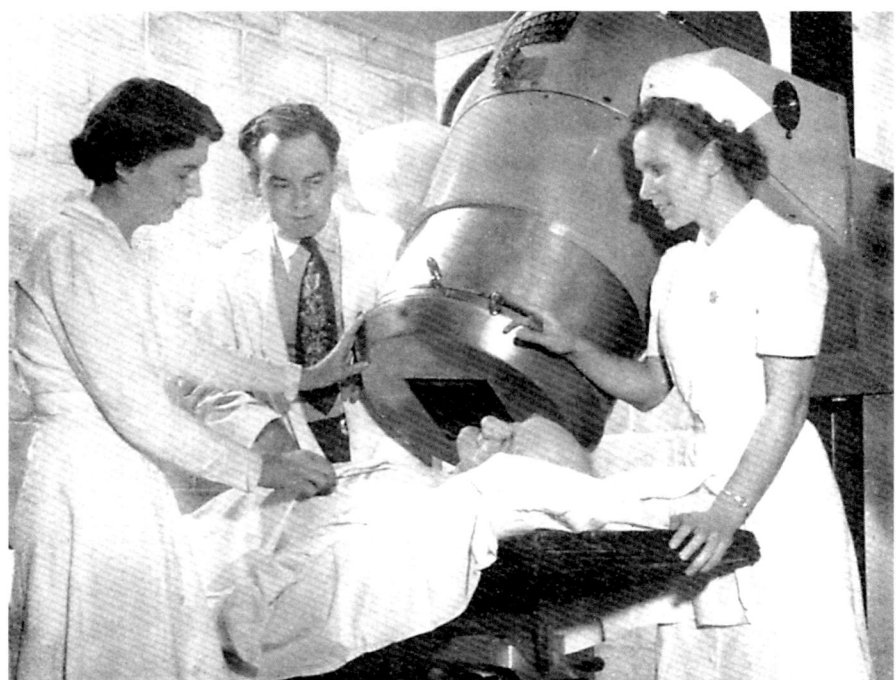

Dr. Ivan Smith prepares the Cobalt-60 Beam Therapy Unit for use, 1951. Left to right: Joyce Lawson, radiologist; Dr. Smith; and Elaine Marshall, R.N.

Officially called Cobalt-60 Beam Therapy Units, the first of these instruments was installed in Saskatoon's University Hospital, under Dr. Johns's direction. A second one was sent to Dr. Ivan Smith at Victoria Hospital in London. Here on October 27, 1951, Ivan Smith carried out the world's first treatment with the new therapy. The Saskatoon unit followed with its first treatment 12 days later.

Dr. Smith, a consummate professional, was born in Manitoba in 1904. His family moved to London in 1908. He graduated in medicine from the University of Western Ontario in 1927 and earned his master of science degree the next year. X-rays from radium had already been used in cancer treatment, but Smith saw that gamma rays, from the isotope cobalt-60, with their shorter wave length, were less complex, more penetrating, and easier to control within their unit. Furthermore, cobalt was more abundant and cheaper than radium.

The success that followed brought world attention to Ivan Smith and London. So much so, that a story began circulating in 1952 that Argentina's first lady, Eva "Evita" Peron, had been secretly treated here for cancer. The tale, although fascinating, has never been verified.

Gary Kerhoulas

GEORGE "MOONEY" GIBSON
(1880-1967)

George Gibson was the only Canadian baseball player ever to star in a World Series and go on to become a major league manager. Nicknamed for his round "moon" face, Gibson was a West London bricklayer's son who rose from catching for a fine church team in South London to help the Pittsburgh Pirates win the 1909 Series. Gibson was a friend of Pittsburgh's superstar Honus Wagner, and managed the Pirates successfully, with a .546 mark (413 wins, 344 losses, two ties).

Historian Les Bronson traced Gibson's early career with the Knox Presbyterian church team, which ran a 21-game unbeaten streak in 1898. Gibson's career with the Pirates included an ironman stint of 150 games in 1909.

Gibson was a hero to Londoners, "several thousands" of them jamming the downtown streets in a huge welcome after the World Series. "In years to come, I know I can look back on tonight as one of the happiest in my life and I may say I shall always be a Canadian," Gibson told the crowd.

After Gibson was dismissed for the second time as Pirates' manager, he returned to his off-season home at 252 Central Ave. (The house was demolished recently, despite heroic efforts by Gibson relatives.) Greeted by his

George and Kathleen Gibson and their family.

family, he soon turned to sharing juicy details of the FBI's killing of hoodlum John Dillinger a few days earlier in 1934.

Gibson is a member of several Halls of Fame and is an admired figure in Pirates' history. A plaque at Labatt Park is only one of his honours in London.

James Reaney

IVAN CLEVELAND RAND
(1884-1969)

Ivan Rand, 1969.

Future Supreme Court Justice Ivan Rand was born in Moncton, New Brunswick, into a working-class railway family. Following high school, he also worked with the railway — as an audit clerk. Thereafter, he earned his B.A. at Mount Allison University and served briefly as a law clerk. In 1909, he entered Harvard Law School, where he met his future wife, Iredell. They were well matched: he rational and outwardly austere, she warm and completely human.

After Harvard, Rand practised law, was a Liberal member of the New Brunswick Legislature, and then served on the Supreme Court of Canada from 1943 until 1959. Internationally, he became well known as the Canadian representative to the UN Commission on Palestine. As a jurist, he achieved lasting fame for his 1946 arbitration award that ended a bitter strike at the Ford Motor Company in Windsor. The award specified that all employees covered by a union contract must "take the burden along with the benefit," i.e., pay union dues whether members of the union or not. Known as the "Rand Formula," this compromise became a building block of Canada's modern system of labour relations.

In 1959, at age 75, Rand became the first dean of the new faculty of law at the University of Western Ontario. He relished this new career and the robustness he brought to it was manifest beyond the classroom — he walked the five miles between his home in south London and the campus each day. He died in 1969 while en route to his office.

Ian Holloway

GEORGE EDWARD HALL
(1906-1972)

George Edward Hall was born in Lindsay, and educated at the Ontario Agricultural College and the University of Toronto. With an M.D. and a Ph.D. in physiology, he became a professor at Toronto's faculty of medicine.

In 1939 Dr. Hall joined the Royal Canadian Air Force, earning the Air Force Cross for his achievements in aviation medicine.

"Ed" Hall became dean of medicine at the University of Western Ontario in 1945. He transformed it into an institution of international prominence by enticing outstanding scholars to Western's medical school. In 1947, Hall became president of Western, then consisting of two faculties, Arts and Science, and Medicine. During his presidency, at least ten faculties or schools were created, and the university became one of London's largest employers. His reputation as the greatest builder of all UWO presidents may never be eclipsed, but not all his initiatives were celebrated. His attempt to create a college system within the university failed and his decision to have a hospital on campus, though a great success, was initially opposed.

President G. Edward Hall in front of Middlesex College.

A strong leader of extraordinary charm, Hall had many devoted followers. But he sometimes acted with ruthless speed. At least one dean learned he had resigned by reading Hall's statement to that effect in the newspaper. Hall resisted student and faculty participation in university governance, and women faculty endured a "chilly climate." He resigned in 1967 after a new University Act placed faculty and students on Western's board of governors. Later, Dr. Hall became chairman of the board of the Northern Life Assurance Company, a position he held until his death.

A.M.J. Hyatt

RICHARD GREEN IVEY
(1891-1974)

Richard Ivey was the director of many prestigious Canadian and U.S. companies. But it is for his charitable activities that he is most remembered. After articling with a law firm in Toronto while studying at Osgoode Hall, he was admitted to the bar in 1913. The son of Charles Henry Ivey, he joined his father's law firm and in 1915 married Jean Macaulay of Southampton. Like his father, who died in 1922, Richard Ivey specialized in commercial law. From the 1920s, he was president of the London Street Railway, which he later bought. Despite many difficult years during the 1930s Depression, he kept London's transit system operating until the city acquired it in 1951.

R.G. Ivey, 1953.

In 1925 he organized a syndicate of businessmen that purchased the London-based Northern Life Assurance Company and was elected its president in 1931. In 1926 he arranged the building of the Hotel London, the city's leading hotel for the next thirty years.

In 1929 he purchased Hygrade Corrugated Products of London. This was the beginning of a long-term investment in the packaging industry that eventually extended to the United States, England, and Europe.

In 1947, together with his son, Richard M. Ivey, he established the Richard Ivey Foundation, and in 1965, with his daughter Lorraine Shuttleworth, the Richard and Jean Ivey Fund. One of its projects was the 1970s rehabilitation of the Forks of the Thames in downtown London.

In the years since, their philanthropy has done a great deal to help health, educational, and environmental organizations in London and beyond.

Frederick H. Armstrong

CLARE BICE
(1908-1976)

One day in the 1950s, artist and author-illustrator Clare Bice went to one of London's secondary schools and was appalled to find several lithographs hanging in the halls. Appalled, because they were so faded it was only by their labels that he learned they were prints of Canadian troops in battle during the First World War. This so offended his personal drive to make art

Concerto of October. *Painting by Clare Bice.*

available to everybody that he immediately persuaded the Board of Education to support a "Pictures in the Schools" project. As a result, hundreds of good quality framed reproductions were installed throughout the school system over the next ten years. Many, many Londoners received their first exposure to art thanks to Bice's visit that day.

Clare was in a position to put his personal crusade into action since he had been appointed the first curator of the London Public Library and Art Museum when it opened in 1940. He established Saturday Morning Art Classes at the Gallery for children, Secondary School Workshops, and the first picture rental collection in Canada. In 1946, he established the Western Ontario Regional Circuit, sending exhibitions to Sarnia, St. Thomas, Chatham, Ingersoll, Woodstock, Listowel, Kitchener, and Stratford so that a much wider audience could see original fine art.

For these pioneering efforts in building a critically important artistic infrastructure in his own community and beyond, Clare Bice was awarded an Honorary Doctor of Laws degree by the University of Western Ontario in 1962, and the Order of Canada in 1973.

Paddy Gunn O'Brien

HENRY JOSEPH "JOE" MCMANUS
(1907-1976)

It's not hard to make a million. It's hard to hang on to it because then you get on everybody's sucker list from Heck to Besheeba. These were the reflections of Joe McManus on his swashbuckling business career. Son of Irish immigrants, Joe left school after grade eleven and was "introduced to a shovel and a coal wagon" delivering coal for his father's St. Thomas coal yard. At 22, he bought an old oil truck and began soliciting business. City Service Oil Company bought him out and made him St. Thomas manager. By 1934, Joe had saved $200 dollars, and convinced the Royal Bank in London to lend him $1,000 toward the purchase of a London coal yard. Joe paid $6500, $500 down, and the rest was history. Joe built a coal dock in Port Stanley, and won contracts to supply air force training bases in the region. To deal with a local labour shortage, he arranged to hire Japanese internees from a camp in Northern Ontario. The young men were happy to leave the camp which Joe described as being " colder than a concubine's heart." As his holdings grew, Joe claimed he was paying 75 percent of Port Stanley's tax bill. He went on to own, among others, Imperial Fuels, McManus Petroleum Ltd., Port

Joe McManus pickets his striking Hotel London workers, 1968.

Stanley's Stork Club, the London Arena, CJOE radio station, and the Hotel London. When unionized employees at the Hotel London went on strike in 1968, Joe walked the picket line with a sign that read, "Union is unfair to Joe." Injuries from a car crash while heading south to Florida claimed both Joe and his wife Bessie. He was 69.

George Clark

BERTHA "MABEL" RICHTER
(1880-1976)

Mabel Richter was a volunteer, socialite, world traveller, outdoor enthusiast, and community philanthropist — a Londoner who is still giving! She was the only daughter of John George Richter and Martha Ann Bullock. They lived at 398 Piccadilly Street, her home for 81 years, today one of London's architectural gems. Her father was the first manager of the London Life Insurance Company, and became president following the death of A.O. Jeffery. After her mother died in 1907, Mabel took over running the family household. To say that she lived under her father's influence was no overstatement. As the daughter of one of London's leading families, much was expected of her. And she did not disappoint. Mabel worked diligently as a volunteer for many charities.

Her interest in travel developed on excursions with her father, and continued after his death in 1932. She was also an avid hiker, and it was reported that she was snowshoeing in London's snowy fields well into her 80s.

But perhaps the most notable legacy that Mabel left to London was her money. She bequeathed $5.75 million to five charities upon her death and established the Richter Endowment Fund to fund these charities in perpetuity. The beneficiaries of her largesse were the Merrymount Children's Home, the War Memorial Children's Hospital, the Ontario Cancer Treatment Centre, and Westminster College. Ninety of her dresses were donated to the London Historical Museums (now Museum London).

Before it became fashionable to be philanthropic, Mabel did it the old-fashioned way — quietly, objectively, and with careful planning.

Suzanne McDonald Aziz

The Richter House, northwest corner of Colborne and Piccadilly streets.

FRANK STILING
(1898-1976)

Portrait of Dean Stiling, 1962, by Jack Chambers. McIntosh Gallery, UWO, Commission, University Fund.

Frank Stiling was an educator extraordinaire. He combined devotion to scholarship with an enjoyment of everyday life, a literary passion for the Romantics and an appetite for the "tantalizingly racy bits of scandal that swirled about his colourful poets" with a penchant for writing poetry, and academic leadership with policy-making skills.

Born in London, Stiling taught school in East Zorra Township and Woodstock. He earned university degrees from McMaster, Western, and Michigan and joined the University of Western Ontario's department of English in 1928 when the student population was 1,060. When he retired in 1963, it had grown to 4,046.

Commanding Officer of Western's Canadian Officers Training Corps from 1943 to 1947, Stiling granted academic standing only when students had completed satisfactory military training. University College then served as barracks for the training camp. As president of the Canadian Authors Association, he championed the rights of authors, lobbying for changes in the Copyright Act that eventually resulted in Public Lending Right, the compensation of authors for the use of their books in libraries. He was secretary-treasurer of the National Conference of Canadian Universities in the critical years when federal grants were channelled through the NCCU to universities, chairing its committee on the history and philosophy of higher education in Canada.

Jack Chambers' portrait of Stiling reveals a pale, quiet man leaning on a desk, his academic gown folded over his arm. In the background is the landscape of University College where Stiling was principal and dean of arts and science from 1952 to 1962.

Arlene Kennedy

JACK CHAMBERS
(1931-1978)

Jack Chambers, painter, filmmaker, union leader, began his formal art studies in the special art classes at H.B. Beal Technical School and later, in 1953, at the Academy of Fine Art in Madrid where he met his future wife, Olga Sanchez Bustos. Returning to London in 1961, he began painting what he saw around him. In the fall of 1963, his work was exhibited at the Isaacs Gallery in Toronto and received rave reviews.

At about this time, Jack became interested in film's possibilities as an art form, creating *Mosaic* in 1964. He gave up colour for silver paintings while continuing to work in film. His masterpiece, *The Hart of London*, was completed in 1968. Thereafter, Jack erupted again in paint and colour, resulting in his first perceptual realism work, *401 Toward London*.

Also in 1968, inspired by his "Principle of Fair Exchange," Jack organized the Canadian Artists' Representation. This organization obtained for artists a modest fee for exhibiting work and royalties for reproducing it. This policy is now followed in all public galleries across Canada.

Shortly after this, Jack, now 39, was diagnosed with leukemia. He received retrospective exhibitions at the Vancouver Art Gallery and the Art Gallery of Ontario.

Jack Chambers, 1968.

Over the next eight years, Jack created a unique body of work, leaving little doubt about his genius. He died in Victoria Hospital on April 13, 1978, leaving his wife Olga and two small sons, John and Diego. He also left an artistic legacy that included his paintings, his films, and the Canadian Artists' Representation, a gift to every artist.

Nancy Geddes Poole

MARION STARK GRAHAM ERRINGTON
(1904-1978)

Favouring red dresses and sporting a holder tipped with an unlit cigarette, London native Marion Errington had a flare for the dramatic. This talent ultimately led to a six-decade contribution to London's cultural scene as dancer, teacher, choreographer, and artistic director.

Beginning with Scottish dancing lessons as a child and later summer dance courses in the United States, Errington began to teach early, and was holding annual recitals by 1923. She moved to Florida in 1926 but operated her London school long distance while performing for the Publix theatre chain. She returned to London in 1928. Within a decade her school had grown to 250 students, with branches in Stratford, Woodstock, St. Thomas, Sarnia, and Ingersoll. In 1938, the Western Ontario Conservatory of Music invited her to design a dance program for the once-a-week student — the result was the first Canadian-made ballet syllabus.

Marion Errington, 1955, photograph by Row of London.

Errington's London Ballet Company debuted in 1939 and marked the start of her work as an artistic director. This premiere included the dancing of Richard Errington, who soon became an instructor at the school. The war years were spent entertaining the troops at local bases. In 1947, Marion and

Richard married, renaming their company the Errington Ballet Theatre. In 1948, it became the London Civic Ballet Theatre, serving audiences throughout southwestern Ontario until 1954. Marion founded the Western Ontario Branch of the Canadian Dance Teachers' Association in 1952, acting as its president for nearly a decade.

Errington's school is currently run by her daughter-in-law, Liliane Marleau Graham. In 2008, it will be Canada's longest operating dance school.

Amy Bowring

EVAN SHUTE
(1905-1978)

Dr. Evan Shute

Evan Shute was born in Bruce County and grew up on a farm near Lion's Head with his younger brothers, Wilfred and Wallace. The family eventually moved to Poplar Hill, Windsor, and then to London. All three brothers became medical doctors, with Evan and Wilfred graduating from the University of Toronto.

Early in his medical career, Evan became interested in Vitamin E therapy for heart and circulatory problems. In 1948, he and his brother Wilfred founded the Shute Medical Clinic at Waverley, a stately London mansion now at 10 Grand Avenue. Here they treated patients and researched the powers of Vitamin E. Their collaboration resulted in many scientific papers that they submitted to medical journals around the world. Few of them were published because of the great opposition from their colleagues in the medical profession.

Evan Shute did not succeed with his peers, but his work flourished with his patients. The perseverance of the Shute brothers was ultimately rewarded in the widespread use of Vitamin E today, although medical views still remain very divided about its effectiveness. The cliché has long been that some doctors swear by it, others swear at it.

The brothers have long passed on, Evan in 1978 and Wilfred in 1982, but their inspiration still burns brightly in the Shute Institute, now on Princess Avenue.

Gary Kerhoulas

SELWYN DEWDNEY
(1909-1979)

Selwyn Dewdney had several passions: his family, education, art, and the bush. The pull of the Canadian North occurred first, and its ultimate offspring, aboriginal rock art, ensured his fame. Born in 1909, Dewdney spent his youth in Prince Albert and Kenora where his father was bishop of Keewatin. His love of the canoe quickened his knowledge of the north and his bush apprenticeship began in 1928 when he accompanied his father visiting Indian missions across the 800-mile diocese of Keewatin. The following two summers he was a student missionary at Lac Seul, which included extensive canoe trips to various Ojibway camps.

Selwyn and Irene Dewdney and three of their sons, 1958.

After his university education and graduation from the Ontario College of Art, he taught at Beck Collegiate from 1936 to 1945. A year later he published his first novel, *Wind Without Rain*, which dealt with the politics of the teaching profession. He resigned his teaching position in 1945 to protest the demotion of a fellow teacher.

He then struggled financially but managed to get by, illustrating books, painting murals, and giving art lessons. With his wife, Irene, he pioneered the use of art therapy at Westminster Hospital in 1953. His overriding interest in aboriginal rock art began in 1957 when he began documenting hundreds of native pictographic sites, often accompanied by Irene and one or more of their four sons. Even after his first heart operation, he continued his travels by canoe. In 1975, he gave a retrospective exhibition of his paintings. This multi-talented citizen died in 1979.

Peter Rechnitzer

Peggy Glass as the Mother in the London Drama League production of Twenty Five Cents, *1936. Photograph by Walter Dixon.*

MARGARET "PEGGY" GLASS
(1900-1980)

Margaret Glass, or Peggy, as she was known to hundreds of Londoners, was a symbol of the grandness of theatre and the arts. In that voice, which could be heard right to the back row, she sounded like a New Yorker who could solve any and all problems of any theatre. She was born in 1900 in London, and set off for New York City in 1920. She worked off-Broadway as a theatre electrician at a time when it was a man's job and saw Broadway at a time of great plays and even greater performers. She remembered all of these productions and tucked them away for the years when she returned to her home. She moved to 603 Queens Avenue, which became her abode for the rest of her life and became secretary to H.K. Baskette, the general manager of the Grand Theatre and the London Little Theatre, arranging contracts, bookings, and productions.

She organized an army of volunteers who came to work in the "largest little theatre" in the world, encouraging everyone she met to become involved in this world of play and make-believe. There was always a cup of tea and cookies ready every afternoon for all who climbed the stairs to her domain. She was also a director and a powerful actress. She saw the London Little Theatre win awards for productions that became known Canada-wide. Peggy Glass left the Grand when Ken Baskette stepped down from his post. She died in 1980, remembered today as the Grand's grandest of ladies.

Don Fleckser

THE HONOURABLE RAY LAWSON
(1886-1980)

Businessman, public figure, and philanthropist, Ray Lawson was a Londoner who believed that public service was both an honour and a duty.

In the years between the two world wars, he built Lawson & Jones, the printing enterprise his father Frank had established with Henry James Jones in 1882, into a multi-million-dollar corporation. By the time he became honourary chairman of the board in 1976, Lawson & Jones had grown into an international leader in printing and packaging.

When Canada entered the war against Germany in 1939, Ray Lawson

Ray Lawson,
c. 1945.

offered his services to the Dominion government. In 1940 he was appointed president of the crown-owned Federal Aircraft Ltd. of Montreal as a "dollar a year" man. The company produced almost 2,000 twin-engined Avro Anson aircraft for the Commonwealth Air Training Plan. He received an O.B.E. for his part in the war effort.

In 1946, he was appointed Lieutenant Governor of Ontario and toured the province investing veterans with decorations and awards they had earned during the war. The Canadian government appointed him Consul General in New York City from 1953 to 1955. Raising capital from private sources, he spearheaded the construction on 5th Avenue and 54th Street of Canada House, where offices of the Canadian government and of Canadian companies were consolidated in a 26-storey skyscraper. He also established the Lawson Foundation to endow universities and hospitals.

The Honourable Ray Lawson died at the age of 94, while on vacation in Florida.

Bill Corfield

W. WILFRID JURY
(1890-1981)

Wilfrid Jury on
the campus of
the University of
Western
Ontario.

From humble beginnings as a Lobo Township farm boy, Wilf Jury rose to international renown as an archaeologist and historian. With his father Amos (1861–1964), he amassed one of the largest collections of Native artifacts and pioneer items from southwestern Ontario and founded both the Museum of Indian Archaeology and Pioneer Life at the University of Western Ontario (now Museum of Ontario Archaeology) and Fanshawe Pioneer Village. Wilf, initially on his own, and later with his wife Elsie McLeod Murray Jury (1910–1993), excavated and reconstructed several archaeological and historic sites throughout southern Ontario. Wilf and Elsie are best known for their years of work in the Midland area, at Sainte-Marie Among the Hurons and the Penetanguishene Naval and Military Establishments (now Discovery Harbour).

Wilf was a man of many talents, able to write both technical reports and popular articles for newspapers. He was equally at home whether talking to his farming neighbours or to politicians and dignitaries. Not a religious man, he nevertheless spent years working with members of the Society of Jesus investigating the sites of the Jesuit martyrs. He also had an audience with Pope Paul VI.

Wilf was a founding member of the Archaeological and Historic Sites Board of Ontario, and helped initiate the commemoration of important places with historical plaques. Both he and Elsie were long-serving members of the Ontario Historical Society and laid the foundation for the Ontario Museum Association. Their legacy lives on through the many sites they examined, the museums they championed, and an elementary school in northwest London.

Robert Pearce

William Loveday, 1964.

WILLIAM LOVEDAY
(1888-1981)

William Loveday, a stonecutter from Rushden, England, emigrated to London in 1907. He carved the baptismal font for St. Paul's Cathedral and eventually, with others, formed the London Marble and Granite Company Limited.

It was when the president of his Men's Bible Class at Southern Congregational Church received a nasty blow to the nose during a handball game that Loveday's life work began. Loveday, who had received St. John Ambulance training in England, promptly stopped the hemorrhaging. His skill stimulated a keen interest among the young men in the class, and he began teaching them first aid. Soon after, William Herbert Pinnock, who had served with the St. John Ambulance during the Boer War, arrived in London. He and Loveday enlisted all those in the city who held St. John first aid certificates, and organized the first Brigade outside Britain. It was officially registered on May 3, 1909.

The Forest City Division operated an emergency hospital tent at the Western Fair, and in 1910 opened a local headquarters of the St. John Ambulance. Loveday went on to organize many other Brigades, and to instruct troops with the Canadian Army Medical Corps in the First World War. In 1960 he was made a Knight of Grace of the Order of St. John.

Loveday retired at 80 after a block of granite crushed his foot. By this time there were more than 560 Ambulance Brigades and 13,000 members in Canada. He died on his 93rd birthday at Victoria Hospital, where he had served as a trustee for 28 years, 12 as board chair.

Arthur McClelland

JOHN PARMENTER ROBARTS
(1917-1982)

John Robarts served as premier of Ontario from 1961 to 1971, marking the mid-point of the Progressive Conservative dynasty that governed Ontario between 1943 and 1985.

That the dynasty enjoyed such a long second half owed much to Robarts. He brought an infusion of new talent into government and implemented a sweeping program of modernization. And he did it so expertly that it aroused almost no political uproar. "I'm a management man myself," he once declared, which was surely true. But it was only a partial truth, and does not explain the public esteem in which he was held or the enduring interest of his life.

Premier John and Nora Robarts, at campaign headquarters, Hotel London, September, 1963.

For that one must look elsewhere. As a young naval officer during the Second World War he had been mentioned in dispatches for his calm leadership under enemy fire, a quality that he carried with him into politics. He was a man after Ontario's heart, a natural leader who always seemed to be in charge, utterly unflappable, and supremely competent.

His personal life, however, was not serene. He drank heavily, frequented the late-night Toronto jazz scene, and generally lived it up. After retiring from politics, he worked as a corporate lawyer. On a flight to Houston, Texas, he suffered a stroke that left him seriously debilitated. Upon realizing that he would not recover, with the same resolute decisiveness that he had displayed in war and in politics, he took his life on October 18, 1982.

Sid Noel

WALTER JUXON
BLACKBURN
(1914–1983)

At twenty-one years of age, Walter Blackburn suddenly became the youngest publisher of a daily newspaper in Canada on the death of his father, Arthur.

With a fresh degree in business administration and a salary of $3,500,

W.J. Blackburn.

Blackburn began a long and distinguished career as sole owner and CEO of a newspaper that was started in 1849. Radio broadcasting was already a small component of his portfolio and later there would be television.

In his time, the *London Free Press* grew from a strictly local journal to become a major Canadian newspaper, and Blackburn became a respected national multi-media leader.

Blackburn was a man of great integrity, who treated his employees with respect. Many thought him more of a friend than a boss. Insiders knew him as W.J. but his dignified, almost shy, demeanour seemed to dictate that others address him as Mr. Blackburn. However, when his broadcast licenses were under attack by the CRTC (Canada's regulatory body), he was firm and resolute as he defended his operations, often under scrutiny because his paper, radio, and TV holdings dominated the London market. In time it became evident that Blackburn's enterprises were above reproach.

Far more than a business leader, Blackburn was fiercely committed to his community and was most proud of his role as London Health Association president in establishing University Hospital, which opened in 1972.

Walter Blackburn died in 1983, leaving a treasured legacy of service. His contribution to Canada's broadcasting and newspaper industries has earned him a rightful place among the giants of Canada's media history.

Bill Brady

MARY CAMPBELL
(1919-1983)

For Mary Campbell progressive change and equality were always goals worth living and fighting for. She believed every human being should be able to live and work with dignity. She challenged governments and businesses, established representation for women where it didn't exist before, and fought unceasingly for the rights of workers like herself. In doing so, she changed London on many levels.

Born and raised in Saskatchewan during the dust-bowl years, Mary came to London in the 1950s with a keenly developed sense of social justice. In addition to her job at the University of Western Ontario Library, she worked tirelessly for the London Status of Women Action Group, the UWO Staff Association, the Committee to End Canada's Complicity in Viet Nam, the Working Women's Alliance, the Voice of Women, the Women's Auxiliary for Auto Workers, the Ban the Bomb movement, and

Mary Campbell

many other peace initiatives. She ran as a candidate for the Waffle Party, and founded Western's first Status of Women and Sexual Harassment committees. Mary also helped to run London's first food co-op out of space in her own home.

Worker's rights and safety were high on Mary's list of important causes. She joined picket lines to support striking workers across the city, and spearheaded the first attempt to unionize the UWO Staff Association. (Her vision and groundwork finally saw results in 1997.)

Mary is remembered through the Mary Campbell Housing Co-Op, dedicated to her memory in October of 1983, and through numerous awards and bursaries.

Roberta McClelland

WILLIAM HENRY FOX JR.
(1909-1985)

On May 16, 1928, at the Arena Gardens in Toronto, before an audience of more than 10,000, Bill Fox, a student at London's De La Salle High School, a Christian Brothers school, was chosen Dominion Oratorical Champion. His subject was "The Future of Canada."

After a civic welcome and testimonial dinner given at the Hotel London in his hometown, Fox received a free trip to Great Britain, Ireland, Holland, Belgium, Germany, France, and Switzerland. Like the Canadian contest itself, the trip was sponsored by the *Toronto Daily Star*.

That same year, Fox was one of eight boys who participated in the Third International Oratorical Contest in Washington, DC. The result of the first ballot was a tie between Canada, France, and Argentina. A second set of ballots, however, gave third place to Canada's representative. Nevertheless, having outdistanced both the American and English contestants, Fox was indeed "the champion English speaking orator of the world," as an uncle and aunt reminded him.

During the Second World War, Fox served as a legal officer in the Royal Canadian Air Force on the West Coast. He became a partner in the celebrated London law firm of Carruthers, Fox, Robarts & Betts before he was appointed juvenile and family court judge in 1960. At one time Judge Fox was president of both the Southwestern Ontario Liberal Association and the Irish Benevolent Society of London and Middlesex.

Dan Brock

GORDON DUMARESQUE JEFFERY
(1919-1986)

Gordon Jeffery, scion of the family that founded the London Life Insurance Company, grew up as many a city boy did, attending South Collegiate, taking music lessons, and skating with the London Skating Club. In Toronto, he studied music with Healey Willan and law at Osgoode Hall, eventually joining the family law firm.

But his first love was music. Gordon loved every aspect of music-making. He threw himself into several building projects, beginning in 1947 with his purchase of Beecher United Church on Dundas Street, renaming it Aeolian Hall. Transformed into a concert hall with conservatory facilities, it became Gordon's musical headquarters. With his friend Ernest White he established a summer school for organists, for which he installed an excellent instrument brought from New York. Gordon's energy was boundless: he created and conducted the London Chamber Orchestra and the Aeolian Choral Society and began an annual Bach Festival. He commissioned Godfrey Ridout to compose an opera, *The Saint*, produced with Victor Braun in the role of Henry Edward Dormer. He also invited another rising star, Jon Vickers, to sing in a performance of Bach's *St. Matthew's Passion*.

When the Aeolian Hall was destroyed by arson in 1968, Gordon bought

Gordon Jeffery at his baroque organ, 1948.

the London East Town Hall, renaming it Aeolian Hall. He commissioned a new organ from Gabriel Kney for it and the hall became a major venue for chamber music and organ concerts in London. Gordon's legacy continues with the Aeolian Concerts, now staged at the Wolf Performance Hall. A passionate collector of fine instruments, Gordon left two Stradivarius violins and one Guarnerius violin to the University of Western Ontario.

Renée Silberman

HARRY LESLIE SIFTON
(1890-1988)

London's oldest and largest home builder, Sifton Properties, was started in the summer of 1923 when Harry Sifton built several homes on Rosedale Avenue, a quiet street just west of Adelaide Street. For over 20 years, he joined a legion of other home builders filling in the undeveloped spaces inside the city's limits. By the end of the Second World War, the city was bursting its boundaries and the market for new homes was about to explode.

Harry was the first to test the potential for suburban living with the construction of 57 homes on Braemar Crescent in the early 1950s. It was a gamble at the time. Over a mile from the city boundary, it was unclear if Londoners were willing to live some distance away from schools and

One of the first Sifton homes, 587 Rosedale Avenue.

shopping. Yet the buyers came. It gave Harry and the company the impetus to continue building westward with Oakridge Acres in the 1950s, Oakridge Park in the 1960s, and then Westmount.

Staying ahead of the market has been the secret of the company's success. When land servicing costs drove up the price of houses in Oakridge Park, Sifton built a series of luxurious homes to justify the price. Again the market was there.

The Berkshire Village development appealed to a growing number of people who preferred renting to owning. Lately, with an eye on the aging boomer market, the company has built a gated community surrounding a golf course in the west end of the city and is now entering the graduated care facility market.

Harry L. Sifton, c. 1953.

Mike Baker

BISHOP WILLIAM ALFRED TOWNSHEND
(1898-1988)

Townshend devoted his life to two overlapping vocations. The first, that of Anglican cleric, began when he was ordained in 1926. Rising steadily in the hierarchy of the Diocese of Huron, ending with his election as suffragan bishop in 1955, Townshend's mission was to ensure that the Anglican church, at the national, diocesan, and parish level, rested on a secure financial footing. A gifted administrator, Townshend thrived on orchestrating real estate deals, designing clergy pension plans, and cajoling parishioners into making ever more generous donations to their church. Until his retirement in 1967, Townshend merged a homespun theology with the unwavering conviction that successful churches require sound fiscal management.

A similar commitment to efficiency and economy informed Townshend's second vocation of public school trustee. First elected in 1934, he served on the London Board of Education for over 40 years. Townshend proved a surprisingly progressive reformer, advocating tirelessly for such initiatives as enhanced vocational training and higher teacher salaries. Rarely was the intersection of Townshend's two vocations more evident then during his 1969 campaign to reclaim the Board of Education seat he had lost three years earlier. He led the charge to have religious education, discarded from the curriculum just months earlier, reinstated in London's public schools. Warning the electorate that, "When you take God out of your schools you put your country in jeopardy," the erstwhile reformer now seemed an

Bishop Townsend and students celebrate the 25th anniversary of the Quebec Street school named in his honour, 1984.

anachronism. But with a lifetime of stellar public service to his credit, Townshend was neither required nor inclined to apologize for his views. He was re-elected.

Keith Fleming

THE REV. DR. GEORGE W. GOTH
(1907-1990)

Beginning his education in a one-room schoolhouse in the Ottawa Valley, George Goth became a man who was learned, articulate, provocative, and eminently well known for his pulpit ministry at Metropolitan United Church. But his ministry was not confined to the pulpit. He addressed political and public forums with courage, insight, and integrity, and was much in demand as a lecturer and after-dinner speaker. (He requested a higher fee if his listeners could afford a cash bar before dinner.) His deep commitment to racial equality inspired him to march with Dr. Martin Luther King Jr. at Selma, Alabama in 1965.

Theologians such as Harry Emerson Fosdick and Reinhold Niebuhr greatly influenced Dr. Goth's thinking. He read voraciously, and peppered his sermons with quotations from classical and contemporary writings. In the 1950s and 1960s, this drew hundreds of university students to his Sunday evening services. He revelled in their challenging questions, believing passionately in Socrates' dictum "the unexamined life is not worth living."

Though he expressed his views forcefully, he was never afraid to change his mind when further experience and reflection convinced him that he had been wrong. He often quoted the famous words of Ralph Waldo Emerson: "A foolish consistency is the hobgoblin of little minds."

His name and likeness are etched in bronze on the *People and the City* monument on Wellington Street, less than a block from the church where he served as Senior Minister from 1948 to 1975 and as Minister Emeritus until his death in 1990.

J. Alvin Boyd

Reverend George Goth in Selma, Alabama, with Dwaine and Gloria Phillips, 1965.

Margaret Fullerton takes her seat as a controller, 1971.

MARGARET A. FULLERTON
(1909-1991)

Margaret Fullerton was one of London's most effective and popular municipal politicians. The daughter of a clergyman, she graduated from the University of Western Ontario and Toronto's College of Education, and then taught Latin at London's Central Collegiate. She married Edwin N. Fullerton in 1938.

Active in many community organizations, Margaret first sought political office in 1953 and became London's first female councillor. In 1960, she won a seat on Board of Control. She was a diligent committee member, gaining a reputation for carefully reviewing all budgetary matters, and displaying an avid interest in planning issues. Her accomplishments were many: the London Centennial celebrations of 1955; the establishment of Victoria House Museum, London's first permanent museum, in 1958; improved status for the city's married women employees; and Centennial Hall, London's Centennial project for 1967.

Prime Minister Lester Pearson appointed her to the Canadian delegation to the United Nations participating on the Committee on Trusteeship and Colonialism in 1966. She ran as a Liberal candidate in the 1965 federal election in London West, but ran second to Conservative Jack Irvine. Her municipal career ended briefly in 1969 when she lost her seat on Board of Control, but she returned 15 months later. She served for only two weeks, accepting an appointment by Prime Minister Pierre Trudeau to the Pension Review Board. She retired to London in 1978.

Margaret Fullerton left municipal politics with a reputation as a vigorous and skilled debater. To quote *London Free Press* columnist Joe McClelland, she had "the courage of her convictions and an utter contempt for political grandstanding."

John Lutman

CHARLES ROSS "SANDY" SOMERVILLE
(1903-1991)

Sandy Somerville was one of Canada's greatest golfers and arguably the finest athlete London ever produced. In his youth he led many high school (Ridley College) and university (University of Toronto) football, hockey, and cricket teams to championships.

Sandy Somerville, 1975.

He toured with the Canadian Cricket team; his scoring record of 212 runs, not out, in a one-day match, stands unbeaten.

Sandy returned to London to focus on his working career and on golf. In the next 13 years, he won four Ontario and six Canadian Amateur Golf Championships. But his greatest glory came in September 1932 when he won the United States Amateur Golf Championship. Amateur golf was then as popular and important as professional golf, and this was one of the four major tournaments in the world. After Sandy's win, London celebrated with a school holiday and a parade down Dundas Street, and the mayor presented him with a large gold key to the city.

Invited to play in the first three Masters Tournaments, Sandy scored its first hole-in-one, and attended many others as a lifetime honoured invitee. In later life, he won three Canadian Senior Golf championships, and served as president of the Royal Canadian Golf Association, Canadian Senior Golf Association, the London Club, and the London Hunt and Country Club.

His golf achievements earned him many honours: Canadian Athlete of the Year in 1932, Canadian Golfer of the Half Century, and founding inductee to the Canadian Sports Hall of Fame, the Canadian Golf Hall of Fame, the Ontario Golf Hall of Fame, and the London Sports Hall of Fame.

Ken Somerville

GREG CURNOE
(1936-1992)

Greg Curnoe

Greg was an artist and a rebel. The anti-art Dada movement introduced by his teachers at H.B. Beal Technical School reflected his anarchistic instincts, which were only reinforced at the Ontario College of Art. He returned to London in 1960 and opened his own studio.

There, he challenged the culture of the day by painting the life he saw around him. He created the Nihilist Spasm Band in 1962 and arranged the great "Happening" that left the art gallery on the second floor of the London Public Library in a shambles. Clare Bice, the curator, was furious and a feud began between the two men which culminated in 1966. Bice had refused to hang *Seated Nude* by John Boyle in the 27th Annual Juried Western Ontario Exhibition. With Greg leading the charge, artists and the media came down on Bice with such a vengeance that he never recovered his strong position in the art community. Curnoe was now the leader of the new art establishment and young artists flocked to him.

In 1968, Greg, and London, again held the national spotlight when 22 panels commissioned for Montreal's Dorval Airport were removed because of protests from Washington alleging anti-American content. It was great

Greg Curnoe in his studio with part of the mural for Dorval Airport, 1968.

publicity for the National Gallery's *Heart of London* exhibition featuring Greg and other London artists, about to tour across Canada.

In the years that followed, Greg became a renowned, widely exhibited Canadian artist. An enthusiastic cyclist, the image of the bicycle appears frequently in his work. Ironically, while bicycling in November, 1992, Greg was hit by a pick-up truck and killed.

Nancy Geddes Poole

Catharine and George Brickenden, 1928.

CATHARINE KEZIAH MCCORMICK BRICKENDEN

(1896-1993)

Catharine Brickenden's persistence in staging a controversial play kick-started the nascent London Little Theatre. A graduate of the Emerson School of Expression in Boston, Catharine "Kizzy" Brickenden got London's amateur theatre scene started in April 1920 by directing and starring in the Women's Press Club production of *Liberty Hall*. Its success led to the founding of The London Drama League shortly afterwards.

In 1934, the League joined forces with two other local troops to form London Little Theatre. The following year Brickenden lobbied the group's play reading committee to stage *Twenty Five Cents* by Sarnia author W. Eric Harris. This unrelentingly grim study of a family in crisis was at odds with the

Catharine Brickenden, 1936.

escapist fare London Little Theatre usually presented. To make matters worse, the play was Canadian. One committee member openly branded it as "tripe."

But Brickenden persisted. In January 1936, *Twenty Five Cents*, under Brickenden's direction, was presented along with two other one-act plays on the stage of London's Grand Theatre. It gained entry into the Dominion Drama Festival in Ottawa, where it won best play.

The success of *Twenty Five Cents* galvanized London Little Theatre, which soon took over the stage at the Grand Theatre and began a run of over 35 years. In the spring of 1945, Famous Players Theatres announced it was putting the building up for sale. When a bowling alley operator put in an offer for $45,000, it was Brickenden who persuaded the president of Famous Players Canada to accept a lower bid of $35,000 from London Little Theatre, which appeared through the generosity of several Londoners.

Nine years after Brickenden's death, a local theatre award was named in her honour.

Christopher Doty

JEANNE C. GRAHAM
(1914-1993)

When she was hired by the *London Free Press* in 1943, Jeanne Graham was the first female news photographer in the paper's history — and likely in all of Canada.

Largely self-taught, Graham bought a second-hand camera in the 1930s and turned her family's bathroom into a darkroom, using her grandmother's best vegetable dishes to hold the chemicals. When most of the *Free Press*'s photography department enlisted to fight in the Second World War, Graham began hounding the paper for a job. After several refusals, she was hired on.

Over the years Graham waded through Thames River floods, defied striking workers who threatened to smash her camera, nearly took a bullet from a sniper holed up in Hotel London, and survived the Rolling Stones riot.

"If we had a dirty story of any kind and she didn't get it and she thought it was because of her sex, she'd be mad for a week," recalled her supervisor, Bob Turnbull.

During her 36-year career at the *Free Press*, Graham captured five Southwestern Ontario Newspaper Awards for feature photography. Among those award-winners were the first photographs of a kidney transplant at St. Joseph's Hospital.

Graham was also the first woman to break the men-only rule at the prestigious London Club when she covered a meeting of business executives in

Free Press photographic department celebrates Jeanne Graham's 25th anniversary with the paper. Left to right: Ken Smith, George Blumson, Jack Burnett, Ernie Lee, Bill Ironside, Sam McLeod, Jeanne Graham, Ralph Thompson, Mildred Coates, 1968.

the late 1950s. When the club's president gently chided Graham for embarrassing the members, she shot back: "I'm not here to jump out of a birthday cake. I am here only on another assignment. See you again."

Christopher Doty

ORLO MILLER
(1911–1993)

The most prolific popularizer of London's history, Orlo lived in London most of his life and seemed constantly to be taking notes, even as a 14-year-old, when he stood with his father and watched Sir Adam Beck's funeral cortege. Usually earning his living as a freelance writer of articles and scripts for radio and stage, Orlo also worked briefly under contract with the *London Free Press* in the 30s and 40s and became an Anglican minister in the late 60s. Not only did both of those affiliations spawn books — *A Century of Western Ontario* (1949) being his history of the *Free Press*, and *Gargoyles and Gentlemen* (1966) telling the saga of London's oldest church, St. Paul's Cathedral — they also allowed him unimpeded access to the city's two richest stashes of historical records.

Orlo Miller in his study, c. 1990.

Orlo is most widely remembered for two books. *The Donnellys Must Die* was the first objective account of the rowdy Lucan family who were murdered by their vigilante neighbours. In treating the Donnellys sympathetically, occasionally obnoxious, but fundamentally decent human beings, Orlo upset a lot of people and even received death threats.

Less controversial, but a trickier kind of book to write well was Orlo's last book from 1988, *This Was London*, re-issued in 1992 as *London 200: An Illustrated History*. As a general history of a sprawling and multi-faceted city, Orlo's final book was a grand summing up of all the stories he'd gathered about the town he loved so dearly.

Herman Goodden

HELEN IRENE BATTLE
(1903-1994)

Dr. Helen Battle was a true pioneer in Canadian science. Her research centred around the embryology of fish and the effects of various substances on their development. She was one of the first zoologists to introduce laboratory research to marine biology, and one of the first women to enter a field dominated by men. She campaigned with quiet dignity to give women a

Dr. Helen Battle, 1977.

more important place in academia and encouraged many young women to take up careers in science.

Although Helen Battle lived all of her active life in the London family home, she achieved fame throughout Canada and the world as a scientist and teacher. She entered the Western University at 16, while the university was still in makeshift quarters, taking classes in such quaint locations as a barn at Huron College, a gymnasium, and the old medical school, graduating with a B.A. in Honours Biology in 1923, and an M.A. in 1924. Her Ph.D. in zoology is said to have been the first Ph.D. in marine biology earned by a woman in Canada.

Her first love was teaching, an activity she began before graduation, and she taught until well after her official retirement in 1967.

In 1975, she was selected by the National Museum of Natural Science in Canada as one of 19 outstanding women scientists in Canada.

Donald B. McMillan

MURRAY LLEWELLYN BARR
(1908-1995)

Murray Barr gained a permanent place in the history of science and medicine through a 1948 medical discovery that dramatically influenced the field of medical genetics and became a milestone in the study of human genetic disorders. His work in discovering the "Barr body," a genetic marker that opened the way to new knowledge of the relationship of sex chromosome abnormalities to human disease, resulted in several nominations for the Nobel Prize. Murray graduated with his M.D. in the University of Western Ontario medical class of '33. After a year of internship in Erie, Pennsylvania, and two years of general practice in London, Ontario, he joined the department of anatomy at his alma mater in 1936 as an instructor.

It was in a Victoria Hospital laboratory on South Street that Barr and his graduate student Dr. E.G. (Mike) Bertram discovered the "sex chromatin" — later known as the Barr body (chromatin describes the material that contains the genetic code). They published their findings in the British scientific journal *Nature* in 1949. This area would grow into a major discipline with the advent of newer research tools.

Dr. Barr was also a Fellow of the Royal Society of London (England), the Royal Society of Canada, an Officer of the Order of Canada, and the recipient of several honorary doctorates from universities in Canada and abroad.

Paul Potter

ALEXANDER KNOX
(1907-1995)

Alexander Knox, 1950.

It was at the University of Western Ontario that Alexander Knox first demonstrated his skills as an actor. He joined the Hesperian Club and encouraged its members to stage two performances of *Hamlet* in 1928. Knox, of course, played the lead.

Midway through his final year, he accepted a job with a repertory theatre company in Boston, but the Depression sent him back to London by the spring of 1930. He worked as a newspaper reporter and honed his acting skills in amateur productions. In the fall, Knox departed for England.

He accepted Tyrone Guthrie's offer to join the Old Vic Company and was among the first actors to appear on the BBC's fledgling television service.

During this period Knox worked with such stars as Laurence Olivier, Ralph Richardson, and Charles Laughton.

When wartime blackouts curtailed theatre and film work, Knox returned to London. His luck changed in March 1940 when he appeared with Laurence Olivier and Vivian Leigh in a San Francisco production of *Romeo and Juliet*. Afterwards, Knox repaid the favour by arranging for the famous couple to use his aunt's farm in St. Marys as a secret retreat.

Knox's Hollywood career reached its peak when he landed the title role in *Wilson*, a lavish biopic on the First World War-era president, Woodrow Wilson. Knox received a Golden Globe for best actor and was nominated for an Oscar, losing out to Bing Crosby in *Going My Way*. Before the ceremony Der Bingle confided to a reporter, "I think this other fellow — What's his name? Knox — should get the Academy Award."

Christopher Doty

Bernice Harper demonstrating a step to UWO nursing students, 1947.

BERNICE HARPER
(d. 1997)

Bernice Harper came to London with a touring road show. When the company failed, she found herself stranded in what must have seemed a theatrical backwater. Then someone at the London Little Theatre (LLT) — now The Grand Theatre — discovered her terpsichorean talents, and she was back in business.

Bernice Harper,
ballerina.

She choreographed and instructed for many LLT productions, including *Take It or Leave It*, a variety show organized to entertain local troops during the Second World War, and a revue, *Flashbacks of '47*, in which her dancers were accompanied by Johnny Downs and his Orchestra. Later in 1947, town and gown combined to produce on the grand stage the first "Purple Patches," with Bernice as choreographer. LLT tackled an ambitious production of *The King and I* in 1959, and Bernice transformed a cast of Londoners into Siamese dancers.

LLT launched an annual summer theatre school in 1946 and Bernice came into her own as a teacher, warming up her students with "Swedish exercises," and instructing them in stage movement and dance. She opened dance schools in London and Sarnia and brought to her teaching discipline, humour, a fine sense of what her students could achieve, and the grace and creativity of her own rigorous professional studies. When the University of Western Ontario added dance to its kinesiology curriculum, she was recruited in 1972 to be instructor and mentor to a new generation of dancers. In 1988 she was named to the mayor's New Year's honours list for the arts for being "at the heart of dance" in London for half a century.

Hilary Bates Neary

JOHN HENDERSON "JAKE" MOORE
(1915-1997)

J.H. "Jake"
Moore, c. 1978.

Jake Moore was born in 1915 into one of London's pre-eminent business families. He graduated from Ridley College and Royal Military College and joined Clarkson, Gordon, accountants in 1937. In 1939, he married Elizabeth Wood, known as Woody, and during the Second World War he served with the Royal Canadian Artillery.

Jake worked on the Labatt's account at Clarkson, Gordon and eventually joined Labatt's. When he took over in 1956, he expanded the company, purchasing existing breweries and building brewing facilities in other provinces, moving the company's market share to over 30 percent by 1964. That year the Labatt family decided to sell a whopping 39 percent of the company's shares to Schlitz. But the sale violated U.S. anti-combine legislation. Jake began searching for a Canadian buyer and recruited Brascan, which ran the power and telephone systems in Brazil.

In 1969, Jake was named chairman of Labatt's and president of Brascan. His tumultuous years at the head of Brascan saw a successful sale of the Brazilian utilities in 1978–79. Now cash-rich, the company became an immediate takeover target, and fell to Edward and Peter Bronfman. Jake left Brascan and retired from Labatt's board in 1980.

Jake's most enduring legacy can be found on Ridout Street. In 1974, he offered his 700-piece art collection, along with an endowment fund, to the city through the Ontario Heritage Foundation, on the condition that a new art gallery be built near the forks of the Thames. The London Regional Art Gallery (now Museum London) opened in 1980.

Mike Baker

MARTIN BOUNDY
(1911-1998)

Music filled Martin Boundy's life. He was able to draw out the best musically in everyone — and that is his legacy. Martin immigrated from England to Stratford in 1923, where he was trained in piano and organ and played in a Salvation Army Band. His organ degree introduced him to church choir work; his band training led to forming and conducting bands and orchestras for the rest of his life. Interpretation was perhaps his long suit and often meant the difference between first and second place in competitions. And he had a keen sense of humour: his one-liners were famous.

Of all his musical experiences, the most thrilling was performing oratorios with orchestra. In 1949, the London Kiwanis Club had a vision of a massed

Martin Boundy conducting a massed choir at the London Arena, 1952.

*Martin Boundy
in the uniform
of the Police
Boys' Band,
1948.*

choir drawn from city churches, with orchestra, performing Handel's *Messiah*. Five hundred voices turned out at Dundas Street Centre United Church to be trained by Martin at weekly rehearsals following Sunday evening services. Sir Ernest MacMillan guest-conducted the first performance in the old London Arena, now demolished, before an audience of 4,000 — truly an evening to treasure. For 10 years, Martin conducted different oratorios with outstanding local soloists, and singers like Lois Marshall and Jon Vickers, Canadians who later became world famous. These oratorios provided happy memories for many London choristers who until then had sung only church anthems.

Shirley Boundy

CHARLES GEORGE DRAKE
(1920-1998)

*Dr. Wilder
Penfield (left)
and Dr. Charles
Drake at the
opening of
University
Hospital, 1972.*

Visiting surgeons from around the world were often seen in Charles Drake's operating room in London's University Hospital, amazed at his courage and skill as he dealt with complex problems in the brain.

At the early age of 18, Drake entered the University of Western Ontario to study medicine. His mentors urged him to follow his passion for surgery, and ultimately to practise neurosurgery.

Drake became a legend as he developed procedures and techniques that provided hope for countless individuals facing death or disability owing to brain disorders. In 1968, he developed the fenestrated clip for cerebral basilar aneurysms, and then adapted it to many other sites.

Despite his fame, Drake was an extremely private person who shunned any kind of publicity. He said that he felt his ethical responsibility as a surgeon was to the patients' care. He did not seek personal fame in the lay media.

Nevertheless, Drake achieved international recognition and acclaim. Shortly before his death in 1998, he received Canada's highest honour when he became a Companion of the Order of Canada. Fellow surgeons spoke of his commitment to solving the dilemma of dangerous aneurysms within the brain and of his awesome surgical abilities. One said, "Dr. Drake was not only a surgeon of great skill and courage, he was a caring and compassionate man." Patients talked, some tearfully, about having their lives given back to them after a complete recovery.

Every day in operating rooms throughout the world, neurosurgeons still benefit from Charles Drake's brilliant techniques.

Bill Brady

CAPTAIN JOE JEFFERY
(1907-1999)

Grandson of Joseph Jeffery, founder of London Life, Captain Joe Jeffery rose through the ranks of his family's company to retire as chairman in 1982. But there was much more to Jeffery than the business of insurance.

Not unlike today's Internet generation, Jeffery was a fully "wired" man of his time. A ham radio pioneer, he often retired to his radio set after a hard day's work and communicated with people from all over the world. This hobby served him well. Few knew of his real work in communications for naval intelligence — that he secretly assisted Canadian spymaster William Stephenson in creating a clandestine British intelligence network through-out the Western hemisphere. For his services, Jeffery received the Order of the British Empire.

Capt. Joe Jeffery, c. 1980.

After the war, Captain Joe steered London Life to full computer automa-tion — a first in the Canadian insurance industry. He also embraced television as a vehicle for positive change, most notably in London Life's award-winning "Human Journey" series in the 1970s.

Throughout his life, Jeffery maintained that "the secret to success is intelligent adaptation" and exhorted Canadians to differentiate between what was desirable and what was essential. This view was most evident in his engaging and visionary 1980 address to London Life shareholders. Abandoning the routine appraisal of the company's successes, he instead promoted a futurist outlook emphasizing the necessity of smaller cars, syn-thetic fuels, solar homes, robotics, and the revitalization of inner cities. For his extensive contributions to Canadian society, Jeffery received the Order of Canada.

Don Spanner

MARIA ROSÉ
(1909-1999)

"Hurry in. We will return to the Rembrandt and Dürer etchings. I will tell you about the Rodin bust later. After we wind the clocks." The clocks?

The days of Maria Rosé were measured not by timepieces, but by the swing of memory between two points of history: the destruction of Hitler's Europe and her new life in the quiet backwater of London, Ontario. Daughter of the renowned etcher Ferdinand Schmutzer, Maria grew up among the cultural elite of Vienna. In 1933, she married the pianist and com-poser, Alfred Rosé, son of Arnold (Concertmaster of the Vienna

Maria Rosé

Philharmonic), and nephew of Gustav Mahler. The couple escaped Europe in 1938, leaving behind their families.

In 1946, Alfred was invited to Western to run Canada's first university opera program. Maria created wardrobes for Alfred's productions, and hosted opera casts and guests with her Viennese baking. The Rosés reclaimed many artifacts associated with their families' earlier lives: etchings by Rembrandt and Dürer, Rodin's bust of Mahler, letters, concert programs, medals, and clocks presented by Emperor Franz Josef to Alfred's father. Maria catalogued these treasures, and made them available to scholars at the University of Western Ontario. She encouraged *London Free Press* author Richard Newman to write the biography of Alma Rosé, Alfred's sister, who had perished at Auschwitz where she led an orchestra of female prisoners.

Maria welcomed guests into her home and into her heart. More than one London family still warm themselves in the metaphorical and material wraps she wove for all who knew her.

Renée Silberman

MARY MOYLI WONG
(1912-1999)

Mary Moyli Wong was born to London's first Chinese-Canadian family, Lem Wong and Toye Chin. Only Victor, their eldest son, was born in China. Mary, Clara, Norman, George, Bill, Gretta, and Esther were all born in London.

Lem Wong worked hard to build a successful restaurant, Wong's Cafe. He was determined that his children would integrate into the local community and have every educational opportunity. They all succeeded magnificently in their chosen professions. Mary graduated from Central Collegiate and entered the University of Western Ontario's medical school.

An outstanding athlete, Mary served on Western's Women's Athletic Committee, played soccer, and starred on the championship basketball team. Her exploits attracted an enthusiastic following in Toronto's Chinese community whenever Western played U of T. She and teammate Dorothy Timpany were invited to try out for the Edmonton Grads (Canada's premier women's basketball team) but their medical studies took precedence. Mary was the gold medallist for the medical class of 1937.

Dr. Wong interned in Saskatoon and London, spent a year at Toronto's Banting Institute, and then returned to London where she eventually joined an obstetrical practice with Dr. Evan Shute. In the mid-1940s, Mary married

Captain Mary Wong, centre with ball, and the UWO Womens' Senior Basketball Team, 1935.

Ross Mark, an engineer, son of long time family friends. The couple moved to Montreal where they welcomed their first child, Gerald, followed by Nancy, the first Hong Kong child to be adopted into Canada.

After Ross's retirement, the couple returned to the Wong's old family home — 518 Waterloo Street, London — their home until they died in 1999, within five months of each other.

Helen Luckman

SAM KATZ
(1917–2001)

Sam Katz, "the mayor of Cherryhill," took the concept of "a city within a city" and parlayed it into a well-planned apartment and shopping centre complex on Oxford Street West. Bowling alleys, health spa, library, medical centre, two pools, shopping facilities, and tennis courts are a short walk from a dozen high-rise apartment buildings. Katz put people ahead of plaster and concrete. Katz once gave a lift to a student travelling downtown who suggested that Cherryhill needed a library. He approached the Library Board about opening a branch in his plaza, a successful venture for all concerned.

*Esam partners Sam Katz and Ewald Bierbaum present their plans for Westown Plaza,
1955.*

The Cherryhill Apartments, once home to London's swinging singles in the
1960s, became a student haven in the 70s. Now about 80 percent of the residents are seniors.

After surviving six years in a Nazi concentration camp, Katz came to
Canada in 1949 and met German immigrant Ewald Bierbaum while standing in an unemployment line. The new business partners moved to London
and in 1955 combined their first names to form Esam Construction Ltd.
Their complex began in 1960 with a small shopping centre and grew slowly
to include 13 apartment buildings by 1976. Katz bought Kingsmill's dairy
farm to the west to provide garden plots for his tenants. He loathed garden-
ing himself, but loved watching nature shows on television.

In 1999, Sam Katz was named to the mayor's first seniors' honour list.
The father of high-rise living in London died at the age of 83.

Arthur McClelland

EDWARD RICHMOND
(1920-2001)

Edward Richmond made his mark only two years out of law school, taking on a landmark fight against bigotry and anti-Semitism all the way to the Supreme Court of Canada.

Called to the bar in 1946, Richmond, a Jew, joined a legal community divided along religious lines. Jewish lawyers weren't welcomed at Christian firms and were usually limited to Jewish clients. In 1948, Richmond was approached by Bernard Wolf, owner of Artistic Ladies Wear in downtown London. Wolf wanted to buy a cottage in Beach O'Pines near Grand Bend. The cottage's owner wanted to sell. But 35 cottagers, including a judge, attempted to block the sale, relying on restrictive covenants that barred them from selling to Jews or African-Americans. Such restrictions were common in the Canada of the late 1940s.

Edward Richmond. c. 1946.

Two courts upheld the restrictions: the Ontario Supreme Court in 1948, and the Ontario Court of Appeal in 1949. Ontario Chief Justice Robert S. Robertson described the covenants as "innocent" and "modest." But Richmond persevered. In 1950, he argued the case before the Supreme Court of Canada. In an order that still hangs in the law office he shared with his son, Joseph, the court struck down restrictions to the ownership of land based upon race, colour, or religion.

Richmond continued to fight for clients in a career that spanned six decades. In 1973, his peers elected him president of the Middlesex Law Association, a position from which he pushed to build the present courthouse. He continued to practise until his death at age 80.

Jonathan Sher

ANGELA MARY ARMITT
(1914-2002)

I may be old and grey on the outside — but on the inside I'm young, redheaded and Irish! This quotation describes an educator of great energy and panache.

Born in London, Angela Mary Armitt attended Central Collegiate and the University of Western Ontario, and graduated in 1936 with a B.A. in English. After teaching high school, she joined Western's continuing education department in 1947 as director of Summer School and Extension, describing herself as "the first travelling saleswoman extolling the virtues of a degree from Western." For the next 40 years,

Angela Armitt, 1963.

she dedicated her working life to helping part-time students reach their goal of a university degree.

In 1977, Angela became dean of Western's newly established Faculty of Part-time and Continuing Education. UWO President D. Carlton

Angela Armitt receives an honorary degree from Western, 1967.

Williams described her as "the president of the night shift." Her outstanding contributions to continuing education were recognized with honorary degrees from York University and Western, and awards from the Ontario Council for University Continuing Education and the UWO faculty women's club. When she retired from Western in 1979, she received Western's Alumni Association Award of Merit.

Angela was devoted to family and friends, fiercely proud of her Irish heritage, and the life and soul of holiday parties at her Grand Bend cottage. An avid sports fan, she was much in demand as a square dance caller. She was also a guest speaker of immense charm and humour.

Part-time students at Western can now achieve an award in her name, just as generations of students benefitted from her enthusiastic support during her life.

Helen Luckman

ELEANORE DONNELLY
(c.1917-2002)

Once upon a time, London's own Pied Piper led generations of children into the wonderful world of reading. A warm personality, a love of children and books, a sense of awe and wonder in creation, and an ability to remember stories were the special gifts of Eleanore Donnelly, the Story Lady.

One of a London family of six girls, she graduated from Brescia College and attended the University of Toronto Library School where courses in children's literature and story telling caught her fancy. She joined the staff of the London Public Library in 1940. The Children's Library had a story-hour room with rich wood panelling, a colourful ceiling, an electric fireplace, and an outdoor amphitheatre for summer story sessions.

To reach a wider audience, Eleanore also told stories on local television and radio. The Storybook Gardens advisory committee found her knowledge of children's books so invaluable that local cartoonist Merle Tingley named her "Mother Goose." She also suggested suitable Christmas decorations for Winter Wonderland at Victoria Park. Appointed Children's Librarian in 1951, she expanded her work to include staff training. Becoming branch coordinator in 1975, she supervised adult and children's services across the city. Graduate students at UWO's library school benefitted from her course in children's literature.

Eleanore was one of twelve librarians chosen to run the library at Canada's pavilion at Expo 67 in Montreal. She promoted Young Canada's Reading Week for the Canadian Library Association. Retirement in 1982 did not

Eleanore Donnelly reads to children, 1967.

slow her story telling engagements, or her service on community boards.

Her story telling magic endures in the memories of the children, parents, and librarians she inspired.

Elizabeth Spicer

HUME CRONYN
(1911–2003)

Although he remains the most celebrated actor to emerge from London, Hume Cronyn's local theatre credits are infuriatingly scant. He was a guest speaker and an award presenter at the Dominion Drama Festivals of 1939 and 1951. In January 1950, Cronyn directed an ambitious but unsuccessful touring production of *Now I Lay Me Down to Sleep* at the Grand Theatre starring Oscar-winning actor Fredric March.

It wasn't until July 1951 that Cronyn made his London stage debut. The play was Jan de Hartog's *The Four Poster* and the co-star was Cronyn's wife, Jessica Tandy, fresh from her triumph as Blanche DuBois in *A Streetcar Named Desire*.

The London production — a Canadian premiere — had a distinctively local feel about it. The set was designed and constructed by the Grand Theatre's resident amateur theatre group. Locals also had a hand in securing many of the props. A four-poster bed, which figured prominently in the show, was allegedly borrowed from the Cronyn family home. With rewrites and a new director, *The Four Poster* opened on Broadway that October where it ran for 632 performances. It later won the Tony award for best play, proving that two-person shows could be artistically and commercially

Actor Hume Cronyn as a child with his father, also named Hume, in the garden at the family home, Woodfield, c. 1914.

*Hume Cronyn
and Jessica
Tandy in a
publicity photo
for* A Delicate
Balance, *1968.*

successful. Cronyn and Tandy later recreated their performances for NBC Television's *Producer's Showcase*.

The couple returned to London 25 years later to kick off the Grand Theatre's 75th season with another two-hander, *The Many Faces of Love*. It was Cronyn's second and final stage performance in London.

Christopher Doty

SISTER MARY DOYLE, CSJ
(d. 2003)

Sister Mary Doyle's lifetime commitment to service is best reflected in her words at the St. Joseph's Bioethics Committee inaugural meeting: "Responsible stewardship demands that daily ministering and future visions reflect both competence and compassion."

Over a century ago the Congregation of the Sisters of St. Joseph (CSJ), oversaw the construction of a ten-bed hospital in London, Ontario. Its philosophy — to value the person and respect human life while carrying out Christ's mission of mercy — was never forgotten, even as it grew into a large, multi-faceted, medical treatment centre.

In 1969, Sister Mary Doyle, CSJ, a visionary woman, became the chief executive officer of St. Joseph's active treatment hospital, St. Mary's Chronic

Care Hospital, and Marian Villa Residential Care Centre. Her tenure saw the inauguration, in 1972, of the hospital's bioethics committee, London's first detoxification centre in 1973, the incorporation of the St. Joseph's Foundation in 1979, and the creation of the Lawson Research Institute in 1983. Long before the provincial government began its hospital consolidation program, Sister Mary Doyle implemented, in 1985, the merger of the two hospitals and Marian Villa into one entity, the St. Joseph's Health Care Centre. She encouraged staff to participate in writing its mission statement, strongly supported the tradition of using volunteers, and instituted the Centre's newsletter, *Vital Signs*.

In 1988, Sister Mary Doyle retired to the CSJ Motherhouse, the "Mount," in London. She died in November 2003.

Patricia Coderre

Sister St. Patrick Joyce, left, and Sister Mary Doyle with Judge W.E.C. Colter at the opening of the Dufferin Avenue detoxification centre, 1973.

CONTRIBUTORS

Christopher Andreae is an industrial archaeologist based in London. He is well-known as a railway historian for his book *Lines of Country: An Atlas of Railway and Waterway History of Canada* (1997).

Frederick H. Armstrong was educated at the University of Toronto and taught 19th-century Canadian political and urban history at the University of Western Ontario. His books include *The Forest City: An Illustrated History of London, Canada*. He writes a column on local history for the *London Free Press*.

Suzanne McDonald Aziz is the Director of Development for the Merrymount Foundation. She has worked for the London Regional Children's Museum and John Labatt Limited, and published *Around London*, a community newspaper about volunteers. Suzanne teaches in the Fund Development program at Fanshawe College and is an active volunteer, serving on several boards.

Michael Baker is Curator of Regional History at Museum London, the editor of *Downtown London: Layers of Time* (1998), and, with Hilary Bates Neary, of *London Street Names* (2003).

David Bentley is a professor of English at the University of Western Ontario, specializing in Canadian and Victorian literature. He is a Fellow of the Royal Society of Canada.

Shirley and Martin Boundy were married in February 1942 at Wesley United Church, London, where Martin was the church organist. They were married for 56 years and had three sons, Bruce, Ian, and Paul, none of whom chose music as a profession, preferring sports. They are now established in business and law.

Amy Bowring is a dance writer and historian, Research Coordinator at Dance Collection Danse, and Founder/Director of the Society for Canadian Dance Studies. She studied dance at Errington-Graham Dance Studios and York University, and she holds an M.A. in journalism from UWO. Amy is a corecipient of the 2002 Toronto Emerging Dance Artist Award.

J. Alvin Boyd, Professor Emeritus, Faculty of Education, UWO, has been an active member of Metropolitan United Church since 1966. Instrumental in establishing the George Goth Memorial Lecture Series, he served on the planning committee from 1991 to 1999. He is a member of the Archives Committee and chairs the book club founded by George Goth in 1951.

Bill Brady is a retired radio and TV broadcaster and writer. His food column, "Bill of Fare," appeared in the *London Free Press*. He is the former publisher of *Business London*, a Bowes magazine, part of Sun Media, and continues to write for that publication. He also writes a weekly column for the *London Free Press*. In 1990, Bill received an honorary Doctor of Laws degree from the University of Western Ontario, and in 1991 he became a member of the Order of Canada, the nation's highest civilian award. In 1996, he was inducted into Canada's Broadcasting Hall of Fame.

Netta Kingsmill Brandon credits the centennial publications of 1967 and new local museums for directing her into genealogy, architectural conservancy, and local history. She has served on many heritage organizations, and as a director of the Women's Christian Association.

Dan Brock, now retired from the London District Catholic School Board, has written extensively on London and area history. His works include *Best Wishes from London, Canada: Our Golden Age of Post Cards, 1903–1914*. He is a contributor to the "Looking Back Over Southwestern Ontario" column in the *London Free Press*.

George Clark is a veteran London broadcast journalist and freelance newspaper columnist. He is the co-anchor of Rogers Television's *First Local* nightly newscast.

Patricia Coderre is an Associate of the Sisters of St. Joseph. She is currently serving a second term as a trustee on the London Public Library Board, and is a member of its Historic Sites Committee.

John P. Comiskey took his early education at St. Peter's Seminary and the University of Western Ontario. He received a doctorate in church history from the Gregorian University in Rome in 1999. His graduate research centred on the early years of southwestern Ontario, the establishment of the Diocese of London, and Bishop John Walsh. At present he is Assistant Professor of Historical Theology at St. Peter's Seminary.

Bill Corfield has written 20 books of fiction and history. He is a retired public relations consultant who specialized in corporate and government communications programs, ghost-writing several hundred speeches over 30 years.

Glen Curnoe is a retired librarian of the London Public Library (1963–1998), the last 17 years of which he spent as London Room Librarian. He has contributed to numerous publications and continues to pursue his life-long interest in local history.

Michael DeKay grew up on the Fifth Concession of London Township and attended Medway High School in Arva. He teaches at John Dearness Public School, London, where his students participate annually in the Lawson literary competition in Canadian history.

Christopher Doty is an award-winning documentary maker whose work includes *The Jack Chambers Film Project*, *The Donnelly Trial*, and the restoration of Canada's first feature-length colour movie, *Talbot of Canada*.

Fred Dreyer is a retired professor, Department of History, the University of Western Ontario, and longtime executive member of the Faculty Association.

For more than fifty years, **Don Fleckser** has been involved in local theatre as a director, actor, and mentor. In 2005, he received the first Brickenden Curtain Raiser Award for his contribution to theatre in London. He is delighted to write about Peggy Glass for this book, as she gave him his start on this glorious life in theatre.

Keith Fleming is an Associate Professor in the Department of History, and the Director of the Bachelor of Administrative and Commercial Studies Program, at the University of Western Ontario. He is also an Anglican priest.

Alice Gibb grew up in the historic village of Froomefield on the banks of the St. Clair River, which fostered in her a lifelong interest in Ontario's history. She has edited township histories of Huron, Lambton, and Middlesex counties, including the two-volume history of London Township.

One of London's more prolific and adaptable authors, **Herman Goodden** has won awards for his plays and journalism. He has also written two novels and one short story collection as well as a history of theatre in London. He is currently working on a new play.

Barbara Baker Graham holds three Masters degrees from the University of Western Ontario. Granddaughter of Sam Baker, she has been a high school English teacher, librarian, and consultant for the Thames Valley School Board. She has served on the London Public Library Board's Historic Sites Committee.

Christian Hegele graduated from Matthews Hall in 2002. The school prizes Christian for his wonderful scholarship, his antic sense of humour, his eloquence, and his genuine spirit for others. He loves Canada, its history, and its politics, and will make an excellent parliamentarian, should his current dreams unfold.

Dr. Ian Holloway is Dean of Law at the University of Western Ontario. A native of the Maritimes, he received his law degree from Dalhousie University, Halifax. Following a number of years in private practice, he moved to Australia, where he served as Associate Dean at the Australian National University, in Canberra. He is a member of the Bars of Ontario and Nova Scotia, and is an elected member of the American Law Institute — one of only 12 Canadians to hold this honour.

A.M.J. Hyatt studied at the Royal Military College and at Toronto, Carleton, and Duke universities. He taught military history at the University of Western Ontario, is the biographer of Sir Arthur Currie, and is co-author with Nancy Geddes Poole of *Battle for Life: The History of No. 10 Canadian Stationary Hospital, and No. 10 Canadian General Hospital in Two World Wars* (2004).

Arlene Kennedy has been Director of the McIntosh Gallery, UWO, since 1989. A graduate of Western's first honours fine art class, she has an M.A. from the Nova Scotia College of Art and Design and was trained in the Museum Management Institute program of the J. Paul Getty Trust. She is a past president of the Ontario Association of Art Galleries, founding secretary of the London Arts Council, and has served as president of Western's Professional and Managerial Association.

Gary Kerhoulas is a graduate of UWO and is retired after 30 years of teaching high school biology. His fascination in historical things is an ongoing hobby and he has been involved in a number of interesting projects. He is married to Penelope and has three children and five grandchildren.

Douglas Leighton was educated at McMaster University, the University of Western Ontario, and Huron University College, where he has been a member of the history department since 1973. A past president of the Ontario Historical Society, he has recently been made a canon of St. Paul's Cathedral.

Helen Luckman is co-author with Pat Morden of *Mustang Tales: The Story of Women's Sports at the University of Western Ontario* (2004). Formerly a member of the Physical Education faculty at McMaster University and Vice Chair of Intercollegiate Athletics at the University of Western Ontario, Helen is the co-founder of Western's Women's Athletic Alumnae. For 13 years she developed and led programs in Western's department of alumni relations.

Born and raised in London, **John Lutman** heads the J.J. Talman Regional Collection and the James Alexander and Ellen Rea Benson Special Collections within the University of Western Ontario Archives. He has written several books on London's history and architecture, and is a member of the Historic Sites Committee of the London Public Library Board, the Diocese of Huron Archives Committee, and a Past President of the Southwestern Ontario Chapter of the Archives Association of Ontario.

Alan MacEachern teaches in the Department of History at the University of Western Ontario. He is director of its Public History program, and the author of two books in Canadian history.

Arthur McClelland is Librarian of the Ivey Family London Room, secretary of the Historic Sites Committee of the London Public Library Board, and President of the Southwestern Ontario Chapter of the Archives Association of Ontario. He has written on collecting local and genealogical materials.

Roberta G. McClelland is an award-winning London-based freelance writer who has published over 100 articles in magazines and newspapers throughout North America.

Catherine B. (Maine) McEwen was born in London, graduated from Central Secondary School and the University of Western Ontario, and then married into an old Westminster Township farming family. She has written several books on local history and is active with the London & Middlesex Historical Society.

Anne McKillop taught history and was a founder of both the Heritage London Foundation and the local chapter of the Architectural Conservancy of Ontario. She helped prepare London's *Inventory of Heritage Buildings* (2001) and is a member of the Historic Sites Committee of the London Public Library Board.

A disciple of Helen Battle, **Donald B. McMillan** is an Emeritus Professor of Zoology at the University of Western Ontario, where he taught introductory biology and vertebrate histology from 1956 to 1994. He is presently engaged in transferring Western's beautiful collection of histological slides to photomicrographs on compact discs.

John Mombourquette is principal of John Paul II Catholic Secondary School and has an avid interest in London's history. He has been president of both the London and Middlesex Historical Society and the Woodfield Community Association and has served on the board of Museum London.

Hilary Bates Neary is a volunteer with written, spoken, and sung words. Co-editor with Mike Baker of *London Street Names* (2003), she is chair of the Historic Sites Committee of the London Public Library Board. Her favourite subject of research is pioneer mills on the Thames.

Peter Neary teaches Canadian history and politics in London and has a special research interest in the social history of the two world wars of the 20th century. His article "Zennosuke Inouye's Land: A Canadian Veterans Affairs Dilemma" was published in the September 2004 issue of the *Canadian Historical Review*.

Sid Noel is Senior Fellow in Nationalism and Ethnic Conflict Studies at King's University College at the University of Western Ontario. He has written widely on Ontario politics.

Paddy Gunn O'Brien is Chief Curator Emeritus of Museum London. She was Assistant Curator to Clare Bice from 1952 until his retirement in 1972 and was appointed curator of London Public Library and Art Museum following his departure. A practising artist and editorial consultant, she remains happily involved in the art world.

Cliff Oliver is a retired secondary school vice-principal who has also been a firefighter, an author, and an editor of books on geography and the environment, a consultant, a teacher, and a lecturer at Althouse College of Education (UWO) and Fanshawe College. Cottaging, reading, travel, train watching, tennis, biking, and old-timer hockey are his main passions.

Dr. Robert Pearce is Executive Director of the Museum of Ontario Archaeology (formerly London Museum of Archaeology), which was founded by Wilfrid Jury at the University of Western Ontario in 1933. Dr. Pearce's interests include the Neutral Iroquoians who occupied southwestern Ontario 1000–1500 A.D. and research on the Jury Archives.

Leith Peterson has training and experience as an archivist, playwright, and freelance writer. She has explored the fascinating lives of Amelia Harris, John Wilson, and Elsie Perrin Williams through her produced stage plays and published writings. London's history intrigues her.

Nancy Geddes Poole, former executive director of the London Regional Art and Historical Museum, now Museum London, is a graduate of the University of Western Ontario, from which she also received an LL.D. in 1990. She is the author of *The Art of London 1830–1980* (1984).

Since 1974, **Paul Potter** (MD PhD) has been Jason A. Hannah Professor of the History of Medicine in the Faculty of Medicine and Dentistry at the University of Western Ontario. His research is concentrated on Greek medical texts attributed to Hippocrates of Cos.

James Stewart Reaney is an entertainment columnist and reporter for the *London Free Press*. He is a member of the London & Middlesex Historical Society and often writes about London culture and history for the *Free Press* and other publications.

Peter Rechnitzer is a retired cardiologist who spent his professional life at the University of Western Ontario and the St. Joseph's Health Care Centre. He became interested in Dr. Maurice Bucke and wrote his biography, *The Journey to Cosmic Consciousness*. He also greatly admired the many accomplishments of Selwyn Dewdney.

Mark Richardson is archivist for the Anglican Diocese of Huron and a librarian at London Public Library. He writes a weekly column for the *London Free Press* and his book, *On the Beat: 150 Years of Policing in London, Ontario*, comes out in 2005.

Jonathan Sher is a reporter with the *London Free Press* who comes by his interest in law honourably — he's a member of the New York State Bar Association. He has been a finalist for the Michener Award and won Ontario awards for his writings on politics, business, the law, and the environment.

Renée Silberman lives in the cultural purlieus of the world. She writes on a variety of topics, most frequently about music. Her program notes have appeared in concert halls in Canada and the U.S., and she provided material for the CD *Poème Mystique*. Renée also produces concerts for *Serenata Music*.

Ken Somerville is the son of Sandy Somerville. He lives in London.

Don Spanner holds graduate degrees in history and information science and has taught archival studies in the United States and Canada. Currently an adjunct professor in the Faculty of Information and Media Studies at the University of Western Ontario, he is also corporate archivist for the London Life Insurance Company.

David Spencer is professor in the Faculty of Information and Media Studies, the University of Western Ontario. He is a past president of the American Journalism Historians Association and a past chair of the History Division of the Association for Education in Journalism and Mass Communications.

Elizabeth Spicer was born in Guelph and educated at the universities of Western Ontario, Toronto, and Carleton. She joined the staff of the London Public Library in 1943 and assisted at the birth of the London Room, serving as its librarian-in-charge until her retirement in 1981. She has been an active member of many local societies devoted to history, architecture, and genealogy, and has published in these fields.

Nancy Z. Tausky is a professional heritage consultant, and teaches English at the University of Western Ontario. She is the author of *Historical Studies of London: From Site to City* (1993) and *Victorian Architecture in London and Southwestern Ontario: Symbols of Aspiration* (1986).

Jonathan Vance holds a Canada Research Chair at the University of Western Ontario and has published *Death So Noble: Memory, Meaning, and the First World War* (1997) and *High Flight: Aviation and the Canadian Imagination* (2002). His book on great national building projects will be published soon.

BIBLIOGRAPHY

Armstrong, Frederick H. *The Forest City: An Illustrated History of London, Canada*. Burlington: Windsor Publications, 1986.

———. *The Iveys of London: An Entrepreneurial and Philanthropic Family*. Toronto: Ivest Corporation, 2005.

Aselstyne, Helen B., and Marjorie G. Ogilvie. *Janet Barbara Groshow: A Biography in Mosaic*. London: 1953.

Baker, Michael, ed. *Downtown London: Layers of Time*. London: The City of London and London Regional Art and Historical Museums, 1998.

———, and Hilary Bates Neary, eds. *London Street Names*. Toronto: James Lorimer & Company Ltd., 2003.

Baker, Samuel. *The Rise and Progress of London*. London: Hayden Press Ltd., 1924.

Bremner, Archibald. *City of London, Ontario, Canada: The Pioneer Period and the London of Today*. London: London Printing and Lithographing Company, 1900.

Cake, Sharon, ed. *Eminent Women of Grey County*. Owen Sound (Ont.): Grey County Historical Society, 1977.

Campbell, Clarence T. *Pioneer Days in London: Some Account of Men and Things in London Before It Became a City*. London: Advertiser Job Printing, 1921.

Carty, Edward J., and Arthur C. Carty, eds. *London-Canada-Coronation Souvenir, 1937*. London: Reid Bros. & Co., 1937.

City of London Heritage Designations. London: Local Architectural Conservation Advisory Committee, 1987.

Clark, George. *Just Call Me Joe!* CFPL-TV documentary, produced and aired in 1973. Written and narrated by George Clark, cinematography by Pat Miles and Andrew Mendham; co-produced by John Sommers and Pat Miles.

Comiskey, John P. *John Walsh, Second Bishop of London in Ontario, 1867-1889*. Unpublished doctoral thesis for the Faculty of Ecclesiastical History, Pontifical Gregorian University, Rome, 1999.

Crowfoot, Alfred H. *Benjamin Cronyn, First Bishop of Huron*. London, The Incorporated Synod of the Diocese of Huron, 1957.

———. *This Dreamer: Life of Isaac Hellmuth*. Toronto: Copp Clark, 1963.

Curnoe, Lynda. *My Brother Greg: A Memoir*. London (Ont.): Ergo Productions, c. 2001.

Dictionary of Canadian Biography. Volumes I–XIV. Toronto: University of Toronto Press, 1966–98. For online access to biographies in the *DCB* go to www.biographi.ca.

Eldon House: A Souvenir. London: Museum London, 2002.

Eldon House Diaries: Five Women's Views of the 19th Century. Edited by Robin S. Harris and Terry G. Harris. Toronto: The Champlain Society, 1994.

Eldon House scrapbooks. Compiled by London Room, London Public Library, 1987.

Kallman, Helmut, Gilles Potvin and Kenneth Winters, eds. *Encyclopedia of Music in Canada*. Toronto: University of Toronto Press, 1992.

Fitzpatrick, Michael Joseph. "The Role of Bishop Michael Francis Fallon, and the

Conflict Between the French Catholics and Irish Catholics in the Ontario Bilingual Schools Question" *1910–1920.* Unpublished M.A. thesis, University of Western Ontario, 1969.

Fullarton, Margaret. Western Archives, J.J. Talman Regional Collection, Margaret Fullarton Fonds.

Garland, M.A., and Orlo Miller, eds. "The Diary of H.C.R. Becher," Ontario Historical Society, *Papers and Records,* Vol. XXXIII, 1939, 116–143.

Goodden, Herman. *Curtain Rising: The History of Theatre in London.* London (Ont.): The London Regional Art and Historical Museums, 1993.

History of the County of Middlesex, Canada. W.A. and C.L. Goodspeed. 1889. Reprinted in 1972 by Mika Studio, Belleville, introduced and corrected by Daniel Brock.

Hughes, David John. *History of the Bar of the County of Middlesex: As Given Before the Middlesex Historical Association, London, by Judge Hughes of St. Thomas and T.H. Purdom, of London.* London (Ont.): Advertiser 1912.

Illustrated Historical Atlas of the County of Middlesex, Ontario. Toronto: H.R. Page & Co., 1878. Reprinted in 1972 by Edward Phelps.

Johnson, Margaret. *Women's Christian Association: The First Hundred Years, 1874–1974.* London, 1974.

Johnston, Sheila M.F. *Let's Go to The Grand: 100 Years of Entertainment at London's Grand Theatre.* Toronto: Natural Heritage, 2001.

Kennedy, Joan Marie. *The London Local Council of Women and Harriet Ann Boomer.* London, (Ont.): Faculty of Graduate Studies, UWO, 1989.

Kerhoulas, Gary. *Roots, Seeds and Flowers: The Greek Orthodox Community of London and Vicinity: Eighty-Eight Years of Christian Spirit and Hellenic Tradition.* London (Ont.): Greek Community of London and Vicinity, c. 1989.

Landon, Fred. *An Exile from Canada to Van Diemen's Land; Being the Story of Elijah Woodman, Transported Overseas for Participation in the Upper Canada Troubles of 1837–38.* Toronto: Longman, 1960.

London and Its Men of Affairs. London: Advertiser Job Printing Co., 1916.

Luckman, Helen, and Pat Morden. *Mustang Tales: The Story of Women's Sports at the University of Western Ontario.* London (Ont.): Women's Athletic Alumnae, University of Western Ontario, 2004.

Macmillan Dictionary of Canadian Biography. 4th ed. Toronto: Macmillan, 1978.

Macpherson, Susan, ed. *Encyclopedia of Theatre Dance in Canada/Encyclopédie de la Danse Théâtrale au Canada.* Toronto: Dance Collection Danse Press/es, 2000.

Martell, David R. "Canada's Peace Bomb: The Advent of Radiotherapy in London, Ontario." Unpublished paper in the UWO Faculty of Medicine, 1994.

McDougall, Allan Kerr. *John P. Robarts: His Life and Government.* Toronto: University of Toronto Press, 1986.

McEwen, Catherine B. *No Smiling Path.* Aylmer: Aylmer Press, 2004.

Middleton, Jesse Edgar, and Fred Landon. *The Province of Ontario: A History, 1615–1927.* Toronto: Dominion Publishing, 1927.

Miller, Orlo. *This Was London: The First Two Centuries.* Westport: Butternut Press, 1988.

———, with Miriam Wright, Edward Phelps, and Glen C. Phillips. *London 200:*

An Illustrated History. London: London Chamber of Commerce, 1992.

Noon, Alan. *East of Adelaide: Photographs of Commercial, Industrial and Working-Class Urban Ontario 1905–1930.* London (Ont.): The London Regional Art and Historical Museum, c. 1989.

Odom, Selma Landen, and Mary Jane Warner, eds. *Canadian Dance: Visions and Stories.* Toronto: Dance Collection Danse Press/es, 2004.

Paikin, Steve. *Public Triumph, Private Tragedy: The Double Life of John P. Robarts.* Toronto: Viking Canada, 2005.

Poole, Nancy Geddes. *The Art of London, 1830–1980.* Aylmer: Aylmer Press, 1984.

Potter, Paul, and Hubert Soltan, "Murray Llewellyn Barr, O.C. 20 June 1908–4 May 1995," in *Biographical Memoirs of the Fellows of the Royal Society of London,* 43 (1997), 31–46.

Purdy, Judson Douglas. *Townshend of Huron.* London (Ont.): Althouse Press, 1992.

Read, David B. *The Lives of the Judges of Upper Canada and Ontario.* Toronto: Rowsell & Hutchison, 1888.

Rechnitzer, Peter A. *R.M. Bucke: Journey to Cosmic Consciousness.* Markham: Fitzhenry & Whiteside, 1994.

Reed, Dennis, and Matthew Teitelbaum, eds. *Greg Curnoe: Life & Stuff.* Toronto: Art Gallery of Ontario, 2001.

Rose, George Maclean. *Cyclopedia of Canadian Biography.* Toronto: Rose Publishing Co., 1886–88.

Rutter, R.J. *W.E. Saunders – Naturalist: A Memorial Volume.* Toronto: University of Toronto Press, 1949.

Ryerson, Egerton, ed. *Loyalists of America and Their Times, from 1620 to 1816.* Vol. 2, 2nd ed. Toronto: William Briggs, 1880.

Sanderson, Gordon J. *The Luck of the Irish in Canada: A History of the Irish Benevolent Society of London and Middlesex.* London, 2000.

Seaborn, Edwin. *The March of Medicine in Western Ontario.* Toronto: Ryerson, 1944.

Shervill, R.N., ed. *They Passed This Way.* London: University of Western Ontario, 1978.

Shortt, Edward. *Memorable Duel at Perth.* Perth: Perth Museum, 1970.

Shute, Evan. *The Vitamin E Story: The Medical Memoirs of Evan Shute.* Burlington (Ont.): Welch Publishing, 1985.

Smith, Ivan H., et al. *Cobalt-60 Teletherapy.* New York: Harper & Row, 1984.

St. Denis, Guy, ed. *Simcoe's Choice: Celebrating London's Bicentennial, 1793–1993.* Toronto: Dundurn Press, 1992.

Tausky, Nancy Z. *Historical Sketches of London: From Site to City.* Peterborough: Broadview Press, 1993.

———, and Lynne D. DiStefano. *Victorian Architecture in London and Southwestern Ontario: Symbols of Aspiration.* Toronto: University of Toronto Press, 1986.

Townshend, Rt. Rev. W.A. Townshend Papers, Diocese of Huron Archives, Huron University College.

Wilson, Keith. *Francis Evans Cornish.* Canadian Biographical Series. Winnipeg: Faculty of Education, University of Manitoba, 1986.

Woodland Cemetery Walking Tour. London: Woodland Cemetery, 2001-2002.

INDEX